PRAISE FOR

# TRUEST
# FAN

"You don't have to be a baseball fan—or a religious person—to glean the gems from this short, easy-read book. Sometimes the biggest secrets of life are hiding right under our noses."

—Perry Marshall, Author, 80/20 Sales &
Marketing and Ultimate Guide to Google Ads

"Wow, great book. I couldn't put it down as it is a fast-moving story that is packed full of important lessons. I was trying to absorb each lesson as deeply into my soul as possible all while I was inspired to hear what's next. The lessons are inspiring and challenging. I will need to read it over and over again to perfect the truths found within. It is encouraging me to improve my life and to help other important people in my life. I plan to share it with my family, my church family and my team at work. What this world needs most is the core values expressed in this book and more truest fans."

—Ron Dickinson, Founder and CEO,
Dickinson Investment Advisors

"I love what the author, Rob Brown, has done. It's just terrific! By the end of the first chapter, Rob won me over and brought me into his story. Faithfully written, the *Truest Fan* journey is an excellent roadmap for bringing out the best in ourselves and others. Don't simply read it. Apply it. And share it with others."

—Reverend Patrick Willson,
Presbyterian Pastor (retired)

"It's easy to get distracted from what's important to us with today's hectic pace. Rob has written a guide that not only helps us reach our goals and do work that matters, but also to get our priorities right and enjoy the journey with our friends and family no matter what adversity we may face. *Truest Fan* gives you simple lessons to find and fulfill your purpose."

—Terry Dean, The Internet Lifestyle Coach

"*Truest Fan* is a fun and touching story that anyone, in any walk of life, will benefit from reading. It is about the journey we all take as we endeavor to live our best lives. The author, Rob Brown, offers seven essential lessons for living and leading with love, purpose, and authenticity. It made me chuckle, it made me think, and it made me emotional. It made me want to be a better person in all aspects of my life. I immediately wanted to share it with my team, family, and friends. Read *Truest Fan*, share the story—you'll grow your faith along the way."

—Matt Ross, President, Ross Financial

"Love the lessons, the texts at the beginning of each chapter, and the people you meet along the way. It kept me intrigued from start to finish. I know you will encourage so many with this story. I'm already reflecting on how I can be a better Truest Fan for my friends and family."

—Anne Carlson

"Rob Brown, the author of *Truest Fan*, shares with us seven life lessons gained from people he has met and through his love of baseball. Each lesson comes with a story, a citation from the Bible, and a quote that sports fans will recognize. This is not a philosophical or moralizing treatise but a collection of conversations that one can easily imagine taking place. I was reminded of talks I had with my parents and others who imparted wisdom derived from their life experiences. Although the book is a quick read, I continue to think about it and expect to revisit it in the future."

—CW Stacks, Coach and Teacher (retired), Charlotte Latin School

# TRUEST FAN

Live, Love, and Lead with Purpose and Impact

# TRUEST
# FAN

## Rob Brown

Paperback ISBN: 978-1-7361298-0-7
Hardcover ISBN: 978-1-7361298-2-1
eBook ISBN: 978-1-7361298-1-4"

REL108030    RELIGION / Christian Living / Leadership & Mentoring
SEL016000    SELF-HELP / Personal Growth / Happiness
BUS071000    BUSINESS & ECONOMICS / Leadership

Cover design by Lisa Barbee
Edited by Justin Greer and Deborah Spencer
Typeset by Kaitlin Barwick

robb@truestfan.com
truestfan.com

To Bruiser, Ken, Jack, Willie, Sue, Lori, John and Patrick. Thank you for your many life and faith lessons. I hope and pray this book shares them in a way that inspires others. Thank you for being my Truest Fans. I will be yours for now and evermore.

To my daughters, Blakeley, Morgan and Alston. I wrote this book in large part for you. Please know that these Truest Fan lessons are the values I hold most dear. They are values that I see in you. And I pray they will be values that continue to bloom and grow throughout your lives.

# CONTENTS

# INTRODUCTION

There have been three constants in my life: God, family and the Cleveland Indians. And sure, I know, the first two seem like a logical combination while the third, a baseball team that hasn't won a World Series in my lifetime, appears out of place.

Let me assure you, it isn't.

You see, for me, each one of these constants has been bound together by love. Not always the same kind of love, but love nonetheless.

This, some may call it strange, way of thinking about love emanates from my belief that we all need to be Truest Fans. Authentic people who believe in ourselves, cheer for others, and trust in God. Truest Fans take every opportunity imaginable to share their love and their loyalty wherever life may take them.

We all need to be Truest Fans. Authentic people who believe in ourselves, cheer for others, and trust in God.

Much of my understanding of this love comes from my belief in God. A God who taught and teaches us to love everybody even when it seems impossible. And though I'm far from a perfect practitioner of my faith, I try.

Being a Truest Fan helps me stay on track.

My family has also taught me a great deal about love. Both how easy and how difficult love can be when you try to live that love every day. Recognized in a simple kiss or confused by the unintended ways we can hurt each other as we go in different directions.

Being a Truest Fan helps me hold onto what's most important.

Finally, Cleveland baseball holds a similar allure. Born and bred an Indians' fan, I have experienced many highs and quite a few lows rooting on my Tribe. Watching games, players and fans has helped shape the way I think about love. After all, with a game that has no time clock, you don't always have to think about what's going on between the lines.

Being a Truest Fan requires humility, loyalty and celebration.

What follows is a series of Truest Fans lessons I have learned through my life experiences and from people who have touched my life. All are woven together by the common bonds of love of God, love of family and love of the Cleveland Indians.

I pray they inspire you to become a Truest Fan.

# FREE TRUEST FAN IMPLEMENTATION GUIDE

Dear Friends,

Before you even begin this book, I want you to know that I am your Truest Fan. I want nothing but the best for you.

My hope is that as you read this book, you become inspired. Inspired to become an even more authentic you. A person who has a deep and abounding love of God, family and self.

My prayer is that you will always live a meaningful, impactful and purposeful life.

To further help and inspire you, I have created a *Truest Fan Implementation Guide.* You see, you are about to uncover the 7 most important lessons of Truest Fan wisdom. Lessons, when applied, that lead to personal and professional transformation.

You just need to be willing to give them a try.

> My prayer is that you will always live a meaningful, impactful and purposeful life.

So, the simple strategies in my implementation guide are tips, tools and techniques for putting the 7 lessons into action.

As you'll soon see, living the life you were intended to live is within your reach.

Go for it!

To download your free copy, please just visit my website: **truestfan.com/free**.

Peace,
Rob Brown
Author, *Truest Fan*

Living the life you were intended to live is within your reach.

# PROLOGUE

Take me out to the ballgame
Take me out to the crowd
Buy me some peanuts and crackerjack
I don't care if I never get back

So it's root, root, root, for the home team
If they don't win, it's a shame
It's one, two, three strikes you're out
At the old ballgame

—Jack Norworth, Lyricist

"Start with God . . . only fools thumb their
noses at such wisdom and learning."

—Proverbs 1:7, MSG

The Boston gathering of top performers had just ended.

Three full days of end-to-end motivational speeches, workshops, networking events, luxurious meals and late nights. I was overwhelmed with new ideas for transforming my business, filled with new silver-bullet strategies that I promised myself I would try and feeling a little bit plump around my middle from too much good food and drink.

I literally had to loosen my belt.

But now, as excited as I had felt to have been chosen again to participate in this annual who's-who assembly of top advisors, I wasn't looking forward to going back to the real world. As inspired as I had felt at times, I was feeling a bit empty and aimless. Deep down I knew my conference notes would just end up on the shelf alongside all the others I had collected throughout my 23 years as a member of the "Achievers Council."

What had I really achieved? Wasn't I supposed to be pumped up from this conference?

And then I remembered my brilliance. Instead of rushing home on the first flight out after the conference, as I usually did, I had decided to stay an extra night in Beantown to watch some baseball. To simply relax in anonymity and just enjoy my favorite pastime. For me, sitting in a baseball stadium (even Fenway Park) and munching on a hot dog and peanuts with cold beer in hand was way more relaxing than sitting under an umbrella at the ocean.

I needed a break from my break.

My team, the Indians, happened to be in town to face the Red Sox. We were scuffling at that point in the season, it wasn't looking like we had much of a shot at the playoffs. Another lean year. And Red Sox nation, coming off a World Series championship, was as annoying as ever since they felt destined to win a repeat title.

On second thought, maybe it wasn't going to be so relaxing.

It didn't matter. I was going. With a ticket for an awesome seat right behind the Cleveland dugout and my lucky Chief Wahoo hat in hand, it was time to head for the Metro to take the Silver Line to Fenway Park. Baseball had a way of putting me in my happy place.

An Indians' win would be a surefire way to lift my post-conference blues. Go Tribe!

As I was settling into my seat though, a funny thing happened. The guy who had been named the Big Kahuna at the conference showed up on the jumbotron. He was sporting a Red Sox jersey and shaking the hands of several Beantown muckety mucks. Seems he was being recognized for some work he had done in the community.

Don't get me wrong, this guy was aces, a superstar in our industry, and well-deserving of all the recognition. But I couldn't shake this funny feeling. I couldn't help but compare my success to his and then eerily feel like a failure. As though no matter how well I did, there was somebody doing more, doing better, beating me, even though we really didn't compete against each other since our businesses were in different cities.

Sometimes I wished I could just turn my brain off.

So here I was, right where I'd wanted to be, ready to enjoy my break from my break—and I was wallowing in silly self-pity, questioning my decision to venture to this game in enemy territory. Then this huge guy with his hair in a ponytail, wearing a leather vest and boasting tattoos from head to toe, sits down right beside me. My date for the evening was unquestionably part of a motorcycle gang. When he accidentally dropped a bunch of popcorn on my lap as he plopped into a seat that wasn't made for a man of his size, I felt for sure like I was in for a long, long night.

"Hey, beer man!"

> I couldn't help but compare my success to his and then eerily feel like a failure.

And that's when everything changed, Bruiser, as I would later learn he was nicknamed, pulled out a Cleveland cap that looked only slightly less worn than my own. He turned, smiled at me, offered a fist bump and said, "Go Tribe!"

Turned out my kindred seatmate and I had at least one thing in common.

Turned out my kindred seatmate and I had at least one thing in common.

A couple innings went by, and we didn't say much to each other when unexpectedly the Indians' pitching ace ran into a bit of a jam. There was only one out, there were two runners on base and Boston's biggest bat was coming to the plate. That was when Bruiser turned to me and said, "Here comes a strike 'em out, throw 'em out double play." Like magic, after the very next pitch, the inning came to an end.

Batter struck out. Base runner thrown out at second. "Yes!" I shouted.

I then turned to Bruiser, reluctantly offered a high-five, and blurted out, "Great call, man. How did you know that was going to happen?"

"I didn't," he replied. "But sometimes you just have put it out there."

I agreed. "You're right. Don't you just love it when that happens?"

"Sure do," he said. "By the way, my name is Bruiser. I'm really glad to be sitting next to a fellow Cleveland fan, especially here in Boston. Where do you hail from?"

"Born and raised in Cleveland. My friends call me Brownie."

"Great to meet you, Brownie. That's another thing we have in common. We both have names that sound like they were given to us by our grade-school classmates."

"Mine was." I laughed.

"Mine too," he responded. And we sat back to watch the game.

The next few innings were uneventful, so Bruiser and I got to know each other. Turns out he was a native Clevelander, still lived there and after a bunch of years hanging out with people he "wished he had never met," he turned his life around.

He was actually in Boston at a conference similar to mine. While my event was filled with financial types, his was more blue collar, a gathering of manufacturers reps from the automotive industry. They were recognizing the prior year's top performers.

Bruiser reluctantly mentioned he had just had his biggest year ever. He had actually done more business, by a huge margin, than all of his peers from across the country.

He was the #1 sales leader, and he had been for several years in a row.

"That's awesome," I said, congratulating him. "You must be proud."

"Thanks, I am." Then he countered with, "But you must be really proud of yourself too."

"Why would you say that?"

"Because we're both here in Boston, being treated like kings and getting recognition from our industries and from our peers."

"Well," I said, "to tell you the truth. I feel a bit like an imposter. My success comes easy to me. I don't feel like I work all that hard. And I get jealous of those who seem to be doing better than me. I wonder if I should be getting more from life."

"Wow," he moaned. "Sounds like you need a fan. Would it be okay if I rooted for you?"

"What do you mean by 'fan'?" I questioned.

That was when it started to rain. As everybody around us started to head for the concourse, Bruiser pulled out his umbrella and suggested we stay in our seats and talk.

How could I refuse a guy named Bruiser?

"Let me tell you a story," he said. And the 60-minute rain delay became one of the most important hours of my life. I remember Bruiser's lesson like it happened yesterday.

Here's how it went . . .

"When we first started talking," he began, "I told you about the guys I grew up with that almost destroyed my life. I'm not sure why, but sometimes I think it's more fun to mention what I've overcome than to mention the good times.

"I guess that's why I still like to look like I'm a biker. I don't want to forget my past.

"I mean, tell me the truth," he prodded. "You weren't really excited to see me sit down next to you, were you?"

"No, I wasn't," I admitted. "At least not until you pulled out your Cleveland hat."

"No worries," he continued. "I get it. This world is filled with all kinds of people, and it's always tempting to try to read a book by its cover.

"Yet, every one of us, no matter how we look, needs fans. People who will root for us through thick and thin. They don't care how we look. And, even if they have to grow on us, we don't really care how they look.

"We just want to see each other succeed."

> Every one of us, no matter how we look, needs fans. People who will root for us through thick and thin.

"Okay," I responded, "but how do you know you want to be my fan? Does that mean I have to be your fan?"

"It's simple," he replied quickly. "It's the Golden Rule: think about what you want other people to do for you, and before they get a chance, do it for them. For me, it's almost like a contest that is okay to lose because win or lose you're absolutely better off for trying." (See Matthew 7:12, MSG.)

"Sounds like a woo-woo concept to me," I shot back. I thought to myself what an odd thing that was to say to a guy with a skull and cross-bones permanently affixed to his rather large right bicep.

"Not really," he said, countering me. "Especially when you think of all the good you can do by just trying."

"I'll bite," I said, "but there has to be more to this story."

"There is," he grinned, "if you'd just stop asking questions and let me tell it."

I made the lips-zipped motion, and he continued.

"You see, the truth is, for every one of those guys who tried to bring me down, there have been dozens who have lifted me up. I have more fans than I can possibly count.

> The Golden Rule: think about what you want other people to do for you, and before they get a chance, do it for them.

"Some who knew who and what I was and supported me just the same.

"Some have never asked about my background; they just offered their encouragement.

"And even more who have done small things that have impacted my life in big ways, and they may never know how profound their inspiration has been.

"Each and every one of these people has been more than just a fan. They have been what I call Truest Fans. They're the folks who live to love and serve and expect nothing in return.

"So, I've committed my life to becoming the Truest Fan of as many people as I possibly can. And now, you're at the plate. Are you ready for the first pitch?"

"Whoa." I squirmed. "Hold on. I'm just here for some baseball."

"I know," he said in agreement. "And I don't want to lay it on too thick. But if you really want more out of life, if you really want to feel like a success, and if you want to learn exactly how to stop comparing yourself to others—this will be the most important lesson you will ever learn."

This will be the most important lesson you will ever learn.

"That's brash," I argued. "How could you possibly know?"

"Because, brother Tribe fan, I've walked in your shoes. And I've learned this lesson over and over again from other folks just like us.

I've learned this lesson over and over again from other folks just like us.

"Tell you what," he continued. "Just put up with me for a few more innings and if I start to annoy you, just tell me, and I'll let it go."

"Alright," I agreed, wondering what I had gotten myself into.

# MY PERSONAL ACTION PLAN

# LESSON #1

## To be a Truest Fan, you must be your own Truest Fan.

"So if anyone is in Christ, there is a new creation: everything old has passed away; see, everything has become new!"

—2 Corinthians 5:17, NRSV

"It's hard to beat a person who never gives up."

—Babe Ruth, baseball legend

As the game resumed, despite our agreement to talk further, Bruiser and I seemed to be leaving our conversation behind. The Indians were batting; it looked like we could have a big inning. We just appeared to be trying to out-cheer each other.

I'm not sure which one of us was louder.

When we finally came up for air, the Tribe had scored 4 runs, including a gigantic 3-run home run over the Green Monster. We both agreed this was a good sign. After all, Cleveland had arguably the best bullpen in baseball. They didn't usually give up big leads.

And that's when Bruiser got our Truest Fan conversation back on track by asking, "How long have you been an Indians' fan?"

"Since birth." I almost shouted; I was still amped up from the rally.

"Me too," he chimed in. "And I'll be one until I die."

We both laughed, gave each other a fist bump and shouted, "Go Tribe," just for good measure. Many of the Red Sox fans sitting around us gave us a big stare as if we were trespassing on private property.

And that just made us happier.

"You see," Bruiser beamed, "you know what it's like to be a Truest Fan because you've been rooting for the Indians your whole life. Sure, they may never stop and thank you for cheering them on, but they always return your loyalty with the hope for victory.

"It may be a single game.

"It may be a winning season.

"It may be a trip to the World Series.

"Or it may just be hope, after a disappointing season, to wait until next year.

"Think about it . . . during your lifetime, Cleveland has never won the World Series. Yet you cheer them on year after year, always hoping for the best, and never willing to abandon your team even when they disappoint you the most.

You're already a Truest Fan and you didn't even know it.

"You're already a Truest Fan and you didn't even know it."

"Well, when you put it that way, I kind of get it. But rooting for your hometown team is easy. You don't even need to think about it," I responded.

"And that's the beauty of being a Truest Fan," he continued. "Once you buy in, it becomes natural. You don't have to even think about it.

In fact, you look for new opportunities. That's why I'm being such a pest tonight."

"Okay." I pressed on. "Is this something you came up with on your own?"

"No way," he answered. "And that's really where my Truest Fan story begins. I was in a place in my mind, just like you. Feeling a bunch of head trash. And then I met Ken. Ken helped me view myself and the world in a whole different way."

"Wow, Ken sounds like a pretty cool guy. Like a real guru. You were lucky to meet him," I suggested.

"I was," he said. "But he'd hardly consider himself cool or a guru. He's a man grounded in his faith and the belief that we should love God and our neighbors as ourselves. He calls that the 'classic definition' of a Truest Fan."

"Where did you meet him?" I asked.

"Believe it or not, just like I'm meeting you, at an Indians' game. It was an ordinary night back in Cleveland where we both happened to decide to go to a game at the last minute. We both bought tickets from the same scalper outside Jacobs Field right before the game started. So, we ended up sitting next to each other.

"I got to my seat first, and just like you tonight, I found myself wondering who I'd be

> Once you buy in, it becomes natural. You don't have to even think about it.

stuck sitting next to. The damn Yankees were in town, and I prayed I would not have to put up with one of *them*," he said while pinching his nose.

"Gotcha," I replied. "An obnoxious Yankees fan can make for a long, long night."

Bruiser continued.

> Fortunately, Ken was anything but a Yankees fan. He was dressed in Cleveland gear from head to toe. Even in a stadium full of Indians' fans, he stuck out like a sore thumb. It was a glorious sight.
>
> Ken gave me a high five as he sat down and I knew this was going to be a special game. Don't ask me why . . . I just knew it.
>
> We introduced ourselves to each other. Then we immediately fell into storytelling and cheering on the Tribe, like best friends, as we got to know each other while the game was getting started.
>
> And then, out of nowhere, Ken asked me what's wrong.
>
> "Nothing is wrong," I answered. "Why do you ask?"
>
> "I'm not exactly sure," he continued. "But you seem to be distracted. Like coming to this game at the last minute was a way to avoid dealing with something that's bothering you."

And I couldn't believe the words that came out of my mouth. You see, back then, I was really pretty shy. I never talked about myself to strangers. Especially when it came to sharing my feelings.

"I'm tired of beating myself up," I let out. "Even though I feel like I've turned my life around. Everything is really pretty good and getting better. I keep telling myself to do more. That I still have a lot of ground to make up from all the stupid stuff I did earlier in life."

That's when Ken let me have my first dose of Truest Fan wisdom.

"Bruiser," he replied, "you need to start rooting for yourself the same way you do for the Indians. You need to become your own Truest Fan. If you don't believe in yourself, no one else will. So you'll constantly be looking over your shoulder."

I tried to break in, but Ken just kept going.

"There's a Bible verse," he continued, "that goes something like, 'When we turn our lives around, when we turn it over to God, we aren't the same. We have a new life.'

"Bruiser," he went on, "that's just a fact, and the sooner we learn it, the sooner we begin to realize that we are all special people. People we should be proud of, including being proud of ourselves.

"I don't mean to be preachy, but, Bruiser, you said you turned your life around. I bet you didn't do it by yourself. I'll bet, whether

We are all special people. People we should be proud of, including being proud of ourselves you're a Christian or not, that you felt the presence of a higher power as you were going through your transformation.

"You need to acknowledge that higher power by accepting who you've become. By shouting with a loud voice that you are an awesome human being."

"Whoa, Ken, timeout," I broke in. "That's some pretty heavy stuff for a baseball game. Give me a few minutes to breathe."

As luck would have it, that's when the Indians started laying it on the Yankees. We knocked three pitchers out of the game in the third inning to take an 8-to-nothing lead. Ken and I were just whooping it up. The only guys in the stadium who were happier than us were the ones in the Indians' dugout.

Ken, noticing the dugout antics the same way I did, decided to get back to his lesson. He asked, "Bruiser, when our boys started piling on the runs, do you think they started questioning whether or not they could score even more runs or do you think they played like the Yankees would never get themselves out of the inning?"

I answered, "I think they became more and more confident. They felt almost invincible. They celebrated. And they didn't want it to stop."

"Exactly," Ken exclaimed. "They became their own biggest cheerleaders. Any doubt was gone. And even though it may have

I'll bet you felt the presence of a higher power as you were going through your transformation.

been just for an inning, it was like they had come alive."

"Right on," I jumped in. "That's what you were trying to tell me about the way I need to cheer for myself. I need to let go of my doubts and become my biggest fan because the life that I'm living is the life God intends me to live. He's blessing me, and I need to accept his blessings with open arms. If it's good enough for God, it ought to be good enough for me."

"Bingo!" Ken chimed back in. "And we all need to let the momentum that comes from the good times, the times it's easiest to cheer for ourselves, carry over into the times we stumble or have self-doubt. After all, no great inning is going to last forever."

> We all need to let the momentum that comes from the good times carry over into the times we stumble or have self-doubt. After all, no great inning is going to last forever.

That's when Bruiser's story of meeting Ken stopped. Unfortunately, it was at the same time the Red Sox put a few runs on the scoreboard and made the game a little too close for comfort. We decided to move our attention back to cheering.

A little while later, we came to the seventh inning stretch. After we finished belting out the most off-tune version of "Take Me Out to the Ballgame" ever, a question popped into my head: "Bruiser, you said that was the first dose of Truest Fan wisdom you learned from Ken. Is there more?"

"Great observation," Bruiser responded. "There are actually six more. Truest Fan wisdom is a set of 7 lessons that help keep us on the track of always striving to be the best versions of ourselves.

"Lesson #1, *To be a Truest Fan, you must be your own Truest Fan*, is just the start. That's what I learned from Ken that evening."

"Okay then, keep going," I encouraged. "I want to learn more and we have a couple more innings of baseball."

"Patience, grasshopper." Bruiser chuckled. "Let the first lesson sink in. Plus, we need to help bring the Tribe home to victory. I promise to share the remaining lessons with you real soon. And I want you to meet Ken."

A short time later, Cleveland's closer blew three Boston hitters away in the bottom of the ninth inning. The sweet victory in enemy territory was secure. Our jobs as Tribe fans were done for day.

After exchanging a victory hug with Bruiser, he handed me a business card and told me to look at the back. it read,

"I am your Truest Fan. You have learned Lesson #1: *To be a Truest Fan, you must be your own Truest Fan*. Begin putting it to work in your heart right here and right now. Don't hesitate. And when you're ready to take the next step, call Ken at 757.645.1525."

"That's all?" I wondered out loud.

"Nope," Bruiser quickly responded. "That's just all for tonight. As it sinks in, you'll realize even more why this simple dose of wisdom is so important to your life's journey. When you're ready, you can move to the next step. Ken will be waiting.

"So, for now, brother Tribe fan, trust in yourself and know that I am your Truest Fan."

That was one game I'll never forget.

Trust in yourself and know that I am your Truest Fan.

## MY PERSONAL ACTION PLAN

# LESSON #2

## To be a Truest Fan, you must learn to put your most important work first and avoid anything that may get in the way.

"Every day is a new opportunity. You can build on yesterday's success or put its failures behind and start over again. That's the way life is, with a new game every day, and that's the way baseball is."

—Bob Feller, greatest Cleveland Indian of all time

"So I sent messengers to them with this reply: 'I am carrying on a great project and cannot go down. Why should the work stop while I leave it and go down to you?'"

—Nehemiah 6:3, NIV

For the next couple weeks, I couldn't get my conversation with Bruiser out of my mind. The fact that he texted me each morning with a few words of encouragement probably had a lot to do with that.

Sayings like . . .

"Believe in yourself."

"You're on the top of my prayer list today."

"Make sure you rock it today."

"You da man!!!"

"I'm your Truest Fan and I got your back."

"Don't forget to be your own biggest cheerleader."

> Don't forget to be your own biggest cheerleader.

. . . were among the messages I received.

At first, I thought they were kind of corny and wondered how this guy, who I had only met once, had time for me. He was a busy, successful businessman; surely, he had better things to do with his time.

And it wasn't like I was a totally down and out guy who desperately needed someone to keep an eye out for me. I was a normal dude with a really good life and a great family and who was feeling some self-doubt. I figured it was a pretty typical bump in the road and eventually I'd shake it off. That was how I handled most stuff that got in my way. Don't think about it, just grind it out.

A strange thing happened: I began to look forward to the text messages. I totally appreciated the fact that Bruiser had my back. He really cared about me, and he was doing exactly what he said he would do even though we had been complete strangers when we met. This Truest Fan idea was making some sense.

When I stopped to think about it, I realized that I had started to cut myself some slack. I was beginning to feel more grateful for being the type of person I had become. I appreciated the good stuff I had been doing in my business, with my family and for the causes I cared about. I even began to cheer myself on.

And I began to understand that the more I cheered myself on, the greater the potential existed for me to become an even better version of myself. That felt like a worthwhile aspiration. I thought, *Shouldn't we always be striving to improve who we are and how we serve the world?*

I had my wife and triplet daughters to think about. They surely deserved the best from me. And if I allowed my almost constant state of busyness and distraction to persist, they would never see and receive all the love I had

> The more I cheered myself on, the greater the potential existed for me to become an even better version of myself.

for them. Rooting for myself would be a necessary step to remaining their absolute and unconditional Truest Fans.

Plus, I had a good business, and as a financial planner, I actually had the opportunity to help others by teaching them how to achieve their most important financial goals. Goals that, in turn, enabled them to live the lives they wanted to live. Lives that enriched all the people and causes they cared about. Being a Truest Fan would help me serve my clients even more.

As these thoughts were percolating in my mind, I became even more reassured by the knowledge that Bruiser was no longer my only Truest Fan.

I had truly become my own Truest Fan.

And then, like he knew exactly what I'd been thinking, Bruiser texted:

"You're ready. Call Ken."

I didn't hesitate. I quickly found the phone number Bruiser had given me in Boston, and I called Ken, who picked up the phone and immediately greeted me by saying, "Hi, Brownie. I've been expecting your call."

"That's crazy," I replied. "I didn't even know I was going to call you until I got a text from Bruiser a few minutes ago."

> Rooting for myself would be a necessary step to remaining their absolute and unconditional Truest Fans.

"I know," he said. "Bruiser has told me all about you, and he said you were ready to learn Lesson #2. In my experience, once you get Truest Fan mojo going, you can't wait to learn more."

"I resemble that remark," I said. "What's next?"

"I have two box seats for tomorrow's Indians' game. Can you meet me there?" Ken asked.

"Yes, I can. Nothing better than Tribe baseball."

"Yes indeed." Ken chuckled. "But learning more about being a Truest Fan will make it even better."

"Can't wait," I replied.

Ken finished by saying he would text me a ticket.

The next evening, I arrived at the game early, hoping to maximize my time with Ken. He sounded like a great guy. Plus, I was anxious to see how he dressed for the game. Bruiser had said that when he first met Ken, he stood out even in a crowd full of Tribe fans.

But when I got to my seat, I found myself seated next to what looked like the best-dressed guy in all of Cleveland. He wore a neatly pressed blue pinstripe suit, a starched white shirt with a tab collar and a brilliant red tie. *Could this be Ken?* I wondered.

Almost immediately, I heard him say, "Welcome, Brownie. Step into my office."

"Ken?" I muttered.

"Yes," he replied. "At your service. You look like you were expecting somebody else."

"Well," I admitted, "Bruiser told me you wore some pretty outlandish Tribe gear, so I wasn't expecting a three-piece suit."

"We all have our day jobs." He laughed. "And I wanted to get here early, so I didn't have time to step into a phone booth and change into my superfan outfit. I hope you don't mind."

"Not at all," I said, regaining my composure, "as long as you're still willing to teach me Lesson #2 of being a Truest Fan, you can dress as you please."

"That's good to know," he remarked. "Let's also bring home a win."

"Agreed." I smiled.

"Brownie," Ken said, clearly wanting to cut to the chase, "do you ever feel like you have too much to do and not enough time to get it done? Like you know what you need to do most, but it always slips to the bottom of your priority list?"

Do you ever feel like you have too much to do and not enough time to get it done?

"Absolutely . . . most days," I said immediately.

"What are your greatest distractions?" he asked.

"Phone calls to return, endless emails, staff members who need my attention and all the stuff I need to do to keep my clients happy." I rattled a list off.

"And what does that stuff keep you from getting done?" he continued.

"Well, I don't feel I'm giving my clients all the attention they deserve and they're the lifeblood of my business. When it comes to adding new clients, my marketing and prospecting takes a back seat. And I have some important changes I'd like to make to my business, things that will allow my team to operate more efficiently and more purposefully."

"What else?" Ken prodded.

"Since you asked," I said, "I worry that I'm distracted when I'm at home. I can't seem to turn my business off. That has to affect my relationships with my wife and daughters. They deserve better. And there's some other stuff I'd like to do, like regular exercise and charity work, that always gets put on the back burner."

"Anything more?" Ken pressed again.

"You know, I bet there is, but I'm so busy I never stop to take the time to really do anything about it. So maybe that's the biggest challenge of all."

"Bingo," Ken said with faint applause. "You hit the nail on the head."

At that point, the game was getting ready to start. Ken pointed to Cleveland's starting pitcher and asked, "What do you think he's thinking about right now?"

"Throwing a strike," I answered. "What else would he be thinking about?"

"That's exactly my point," Ken continued.

"He's thinking about the most important thing he needs to do at this very moment. Even though there are distractions all around him, he's focusing on what matters the most.

Even though there are distractions all around him, he's focusing on what matters the most.

"Sure, he may be drawing energy from the fans. And he's making sure his teammates are in the right spots. But more than anything else, he's thinking about the most important job he has to do at this very moment.

"On top of that, he's going to try to stay in the moment for as long as he's on the mound because he knows distractions are his enemies. If he lets other thoughts get into his head, he won't have the focus and energy he needs to throw the right pitch. Pitch after pitch. Batter after batter. Inning after inning."

"Don't you think that's a little overkill?" I asked. "He's won two Cy Young Awards; he doesn't have to grind that much."

"Exactly the opposite." Ken shot back quickly. "It's his ability to stay in the moment, put first things first, that makes him such a great pitcher.

"On top of that, preparing to be ready to be in the zone is one of the most important aspects of his training. Whether he's lifting weights, working on cardio or practicing his mental game, he's thinking about how he's going to stay in the moment on the mound.

"In his view, he has very important work to do, and he's not going to let anything else get in the way."

"Does that have anything to do with your questions about my distractions?" I asked.

"Brownie," he said, "it has absolutely everything to do with you and the reason we're here tonight. In fact, it's Lesson #2 of Truest Fan Wisdom: *To be a Truest Fan, you must learn to put your most important work first and avoid anything that may get in the way.*"

"I think I understand," I remarked. "Please tell me more."

"You see," Ken cheerfully continued, "we live in a world where it's easy to put other people's agendas ahead of our own. When we allow

> He has very important work to do, and he's not going to let anything else get in the way.

ourselves to become distracted by text messages, emails and phone calls, we are surrendering our time to others.

"When we decide on our priorities at work or at home or on causes we care about, we're planning to put them ahead of other things we could be working on. Yet, new ideas, silver bullets and other common distractions of life often interrupt us. And each time we allow that to happen, we're saying, at least subconsciously, that the distraction is more important than the priority.

"Sometimes those distractions are important, but we need to consciously decide whether we need to move them ahead of our current priorities. If we do, that becomes our important work. And we may have to set something aside that we had previously undertaken. Most often, we just need to plan a time in the future to take on that important distraction.

"Let me give you some quick examples. You mentioned that at work marketing, bringing in new clients, is an important part of your responsibilities, but it often gets pushed aside by the busyness of the day. If it's truly critical to your success, you need to make it a priority. Like concentrating on throwing strikes.

"You also mentioned that sometimes you feel distracted at home. That's a sure sign that you're avoiding or ignoring the important work of being a husband and father. That doesn't

> When we allow ourselves to become distracted by text messages, emails and phone calls, we are surrendering our time to others.

make you a bad guy, but you'll never win the Cy Young at home. If that's an achievement worth going after, you must make your time at home a priority and put aside the things that are keeping you from being your best."

"That's harsh," I cut in, "but I get it. Life is full of choices and we all need to decide whether or not we're going to put our most important priorities ahead of our daily distractions."

"I couldn't have said it any better myself," Ken replied. "But I'd like to add a quote from one of my favorite time-management experts: 'I'm doing a great work; I can't come down.' That's what Nehemiah said in the Old Testament when his enemies were trying to keep him from rebuilding the wall around Jerusalem. He knew he was doing important work for God.

I'm doing a great work; I can't come down.

"His distractors, who had their own priorities, wanted him to come down from the wall to meet with them. Probably to kill him. And Nehemiah repeated four times that he was doing important work and he would not be distracted and come down.

"He finished rebuilding the wall, which had originally taken many years to build, in just 52 days. That was an amazing feat."

"Wow, I never thought about that Bible story that way before, but you're absolutely right," I said. "When we begin to truly understand and focus on what's most important in our lives, God is usually behind the scenes helping us set our direction. So, when we get distracted, we run the risk of missing out on God's plans for our lives."

"Preach it, brother," Ken laughed. "You now know the secret of Lesson #2. *You must learn to put your most important work first and avoid anything that may get in the way.*"

As we continued to watch the game, I had a new appreciation for the way it's played. Individually and collectively, the players and coaches have to be willing to put what's most important first or they risk losing. They must keep their focus between the lines.

I started to think about the distractions that could come from the loud noises of obnoxious fans booing them loudly or from thoughts of the latest press clippings detailing a batting slump that had been going on for weeks. I thought about the aches and pains that come from being a professional athlete.

And I thought about the fact that each one of these guys had a family, just like the rest of us. As sons, husbands and fathers, they were subject to the same thoughts and emotions. Stuff that can distract you even when you're in the middle of an important meeting or trying to meet an impending deadline.

Fortunately, on that night, Cleveland's ace did not come down from his wall. Even though he struggled with his control at times and gave up 5 walks, he ended up with a complete game shutout. But I also realized, thanks to some dazzling defensive plays, the win required a bunch of other guys to stay focused as well. They had to do their important work in the field.

As we were saying our goodbyes, Ken asked, "What are you going to do with Lesson #2? Learning the rule is essential, but putting it into action gets the results."

"I know. I know," I said. "I'm ready to take it head on. First, I'm going to dedicate some time to carefully choosing my priorities by thinking of each of them as important work . . . as one of my walls.

"Then I'm also going to make a list of the stuff that might normally tempt me to come down from my walls . . . my normal distractions.

"And finally, I'm going to try my best to remind myself of my important work each and every day. . . . Repetition is going to be critical."

"That's a winning game plan," Ken reassured me. "And don't forget, I'm your Truest Fan. if you need some help, I'm here for you."

"Thanks, Ken. I know you will be," I said. "But I have to wonder . . . what's next?"

Learning the rule is essential, but putting it into action gets the results.

"As the old saying goes," Ken chuckled like a wise philosopher, "when the student is ready, the teacher will appear."

## MY PERSONAL ACTION PLAN

# LESSON #3

## Love one another because no matter whether you win or lose, life is about the way you play the game.

"You are the light of the world. A town built on a hill cannot be hidden. Neither do people light a lamp and put it under a bowl. Instead they put it on its stand, and it gives light to everyone in the house. In the same way, let your light shine before others, that they may see your good deeds and glorify your Father in heaven."

—Matthew 5:14–16, NIV

"For when the great scorer comes to write against your name, He marks not that you won or lost but how you played the game."

—Grantland Rice, sports writing legend

For the next few weeks, Bruiser's daily text messages were replaced by messages from Ken . . .

"You have important work to do."

"What really matters most?"

"Is anything getting in your way today?"

"Make sure you put time with yourself on your calendar."

"Don't be afraid to say no."

"Just because it's not important today doesn't mean you won't get to it in the future."

"Plan the plan."

"Success doesn't usually come in a day. . . . It's the result of daily consistency."

"Just focus."

"Are you staying on top of your walls?"

> Success doesn't usually come in a day. . . . It's the result of daily consistency.

. . . and I couldn't remember a more productive period in my life. I felt like I was in the proverbial zone. Operating on all cylinders. Work-life balance was actually balanced. And best of all, people noticed.

Clients, coworkers, family and even the people on committees I served on at church—folks wondered where I had found my happy pills. They looked at me like you look at someone who has lost a bunch of weight, but because you see them all the time and the change has been steady, you're afraid to say something.

The one person who absolutely wasn't afraid to say anything was my wife. Even though I hadn't yet begun to share my encounters with Bruiser and Ken with her, she noticed something different about me. One evening while lying in bed, as we were saying our goodnights, she suddenly grabbed me, gave me a huge hug and said, "I'm proud of you. You've always been a terrific husband, father and provider, but you've upped your game and I couldn't love you any more than I do right now. Thank you for being you."

Thank you for being you.

I couldn't think of anything to say in reply and I could tell she didn't need me to. My subtle transformation now seemed almost tangible. I slept really well that night. The peace I felt was like a warm blanket.

As I awoke the next morning, it dawned on me: "My wife is my Truest Fan." By being my own Truest Fan and learning to focus on the stuff that mattered most, I was gaining new fans with greater love and loyalty even if they didn't think of themselves that way. Even if they hadn't learned the Truest Fan wisdom

I had gained from meeting Bruiser and Ken and taking the chance of putting it into action.

Then, like he was reading my mind, Ken texted me, "You're ready for Lesson #3. Jack can't wait to meet you. He's saving you a seat in his luxury suite for Sunday's game. Bring your glove."

I jokingly texted back, "Are you telling me I need to come down from my wall?"

"Yes, important work," Ken shot back. "Don't be such a wise guy."

Moments later, Jack messaged me with my ticket for the game. I was excited. I had never been in the luxury suites, and I was due for some more Truest Fan wisdom. Sunday could not have gotten there soon enough.

And then another message came: "Come early. Glove required."

What did Jack have in store for me?

The weather on game day was perfect. Sunny, not too hot, and a gentle breeze was coming in from Lake Erie from straight away center field.

As I arrived at the suite, a man dressed in a full Cleveland uniform tossed me a ball. "Hurry up, Brownie," he shouted. "They're waiting for us on the field."

"J-J-Jack???" I stammered. "Did you say on the field?"

"Yes, let's go. I'll explain later."

And then Jack whisked me into an elevator that opened in a tunnel that led to a small gate directly behind home plate. One of my wildest dreams was coming true. I was about to step on the same turf my boyhood heroes had called home.

If Jack was saying anything to me, I don't remember a word.

Next, we were escorted to the grass in right field where a small group of what looked like grade schoolers were gathered with the team's mascot, Slider. They were all high-fiving and taking pictures.

Suddenly, everything stopped as the kids pounced on Jack, almost tackling him to the ground, shouting for a game of catch. Jack reached into a small bag he had strung over his shoulder, pulled out a few balls, and the next thing you knew we were all playing an orderly and ordinary game of catch like right field had been our home for years. Like kids playing in our own backyards.

At first, I was tossing a ball back and forth with a sweet little girl. She was freckled, ponytailed, wearing a Chief Wahoo t-shirt and sporting a mean black eye. She would return my soft tosses with fastballs right down the middle. I quickly learned I didn't need to baby her; she could more than hold her own in a game of catch.

About five minutes into our game, Jack asked everyone to switch partners. He and I ended up tossing the ball back and forth. Like I was twelve years old all over again, we started calling pitches, faking high flies and fielding grounders. I didn't want it to end.

As we noticed more and more players coming out to the outfield to stretch and run sprints, Jack shouted out, "Gather around kids, one more treat before we head back upstairs."

Then, like Superman flying in from the sky, my favorite player, Cleveland's first baseman, joined our circle giving each one of us a fist bump. He thanked each one of us for coming out to the game and sheepishly agreed, at the encouragement of one of the kids, that he would hit a home run for us that day.

Before he walked away, he asked me if I was Jack. I said no and pointed to the real Jack. That's when Jack was swallowed up by a bear hug from the first baseman. Then they exchanged words none of us could hear.

> There is nothing more important than the love you show for one another.

As the embrace ended, our All-Star corner infielder smiled with a grin that went from ear to ear and said, "Kids, there is nothing more important than the love you show for one another. So, remember, in life, it's not whether you win or lose, it's how you play the game. Jack knows that as well as anyone I have ever met."

*Funny,* I thought. *A few minutes ago, these two men had obviously never met. And now, a guy I respect a lot, not only as a player, but also for the work he had done in the community, paid Jack a compliment of the highest order.* I couldn't wait to learn more, to learn Lesson #3.

As Jack, the kids and I rode the elevator back to suite level, I could only think that this would be one of my greatest days ever at an Indians' game and they still hadn't finished painting the lines on the field. Who was Jack? What was he going to teach me?

The only words I remember saying in that moment were, "Jack, did you know that was my favorite Indian?"

He didn't answer me.

Once inside the suite, Jack pulled me aside and suggested it should quiet down for a little while so this would be a good time for the two of us to talk.

He started. "I bet you have a million questions. I'll try to answer every one of them. But I have to admit, I'm still kind of speechless after what we just heard. I wouldn't have expected that in a million years."

Then, like a clock wound too tightly, Jack's speechlessness ended.

"Brownie," he started, "I don't normally watch Cleveland games from the luxury suites. I've never been on the field before. And I've never, ever met one of the players in person. But today, that all happened.

"And what's even more amazing, even though you don't yet know it, you got to learn Truest Fan Lesson #3 from your favorite player. I couldn't have scripted that message any better.

"Lesson #3 of Truest Fan wisdom is *Love one another because no matter whether you win or lose, life is about the way you play the game.*"

"Incredible," I said, trying to sneak in a few words.

Jack then continued with a tale of how this event came together.

"About six years ago, I lost my son, Jimmy, in an awful car accident. I thought my life was over. But one day, when I returned to the hospital where Jimmy had spent the last few weeks of his life, a little boy stopped me. He knew I was picking up Jimmy's things. He wanted to give me Jimmy's baseball mitt, he had been innocently borrowing it since it had been left behind.

"As he reached out to hand the glove to me, he told me how sorry he was that Jimmy wasn't going to go home, and how lucky he felt because he was going to be able to go back to live with his friends at a children's home.

"When I told him that he could keep the mitt, my sadness went away for a few minutes because I knew that's what Jimmy would want me to do. I also thought how both strange and sweet it was that this boy was looking forward to going back to an orphanage.

"Don't get me wrong, as I left the hospital, I was still mad as hell about losing my son in a senseless accident. But I also got a glimpse of something I wanted to figure out. Although it wasn't as clear as it is today, I was beginning my Truest Fan journey.

"Fast forward about 9 months. I read a story in the Cleveland *Plain Dealer* about a children's home the Indians' organization was supporting through their foundation. I wondered if it was the same place the little boy in the hospital had mentioned. I decided to visit and see if there was a way I could help.

"As good luck and a probable nudge from God would have it, the first person I saw when I walked into the children's home was the little boy from the hospital. He immediately walked up to me and thanked me again for the baseball glove. He told me it had helped him become the best shortstop in the home.

"My heart was filled with joy. Something good had come from Jimmy's death. At that point, I was determined to become a cheerleader for all the kids in this place they called home. I didn't do it to get anything in return. I just knew that by teaching, playing with and loving these kids, their lives would be better. My corner of the world would be safer, happier and stronger than before I had become a volunteer.

"My game had been unexpectedly and permanently changed. But only I could decide how to play it. I was going to give it my best.

"Now that brings me to today's game. I received an anonymous letter offering me a suite to this game and a chance to play catch on the field. I could bring the kids as well as two chaperones. Everything we eat and drink is free.

"Scott over there is one of the chaperones. Ken was going to be one too until he told me you'd be the perfect man for the job. So far, you're doing okay."

As I looked around the suite at all the kids, my head was still buzzing. I was struggling to take it all in, but I had to say something. "Sounds like you deserve everything you've gotten today. You're an amazing man."

My game had been unexpectedly and permanently changed. But only I could decide how to play it. I was going to give it my best.

"Hold on," Jack cut me off quickly. "This isn't for me, it's for the kids. I've just been fortunate enough, like you, to be along for the ride."

"Sorry," I apologized, "that didn't come out the way I intended. I guess what I was trying to say is that sometimes when you love people with all of your heart, when you do things the way they're really supposed to be done, there's a boomerang effect. The joy you share bounces right back at you."

"Much better," Jack said in approval. "Ken said you were a fast learner. Being a Truest Fan has its benefits, but they come from being in a position to give. Not by what you expect or even sometimes what you get in return.

"We're not meant to do things just so others can see us. We're really built so that others see God through the things that we do. When we trust God that way, the transformation we experience and the good gifts that we share are multiplied exponentially.

"Working with these kids and giving as much as I can to others is the light that has come from the darkness of losing Jimmy."

We were quiet for quite some time after that exchange. We were watching, but not really watching, the game. The lesson we were sharing was humbling. God, working through ordinary human beings, can do miracles.

We're not meant to do things just so others can see us. We're really built so that others see God through the things that we do.

The health, happiness and hope that the kids we were at the game with was a miracle. The result of those kids having Truest Fans, like Jack, in their lives.

Our silence was broken by a thunderous cheer. The Indians had just hit a grand slam home run to take a commanding lead. When Jack and I looked at the scoreboard to see who hit the home run, we were not surprised.

"He's the one who sent you the invitation," I suggested.

"No doubt," Jack grinned.

We went back to our chaperone duties and finished another Indians' victory while sharing lots of peanuts, cotton candy and hot dogs with the kids. Ballpark food never tasted so good.

As the top of the ninth inning got underway, Jack and I rejoined our conversation. With such a big lead, we knew our remaining time together would be short.

"Jack," I began, "thank you for teaching me Lesson #3. Even though it's a lesson I've probably known for much of my life, it's easy to forget."

"True that," Jack said. "The coolest thing about being a Truest Fan is that it only requires we consciously live the way we were built to live."

The coolest thing about being a Truest Fan is that it only requires we consciously live the way we were built to live.

"Consciously, that's a big part of it," I echoed.

"So, go and do likewise," Jack prodded.

"I will," I said confidently, "and I won't even ask when I'll get to the next Truest Fan lesson."

Jack just winked.

# MY PERSONAL ACTION PLAN

# LESSON #4

## Smiles and kind words go a long way. When you're a Truest Fan, you're always on duty.

"He has told you, O mortal, what is good; and what does the Lord require of you but to do justice, and to love kindness, and to walk humbly with your God?"

—Micah 6:8, NRSV

"You could be a kid for as long as you want when you play baseball."

—Cal Ripken Jr., Hall of Fame shortstop

As you can probably guess by now, Ken's daily text messages were replaced by a steady dose of cheerleading from Jack . . .

"It's a great day to play . . . play your best!"

"Are you making a difference today?"

"Go ahead, share some love."

"Are you making people smile?"

"He made you so he could love you, don't forget to hold up your end of the deal."

"Are you being the best Truest Fan you can be?"

Are you being the best Truest Fan you can be?

. . . and each day I could feel my confidence growing. I was increasingly convinced that by rooting for myself, focusing on what was important and playing the game the way it was meant to be played, my life was going to be different.

When I had previously thought about the concept of transformation, it seemed foreign. Like something only those new age yoga types thought possible. But here I was transforming. And not by making any radical changes. By just intentionally living the way I deep inside knew I was supposed to live.

It was amazing; getting out of bed in the morning was now easier than it had ever been. Each new day was like an adventure. I felt energized and ready to meet it head on.

At home, my family time, which had always been precious, felt more alive. Instead of trying to squeeze my wife and daughters into my work routines, I planned for ways to be with them. I literally put them on my calendar.

My Saturday-morning dates for breakfast with my daughters became one of the highlights of our weeks. We loved being with each other without their mother listening in. Their smiles and laughter were like a huge shot of adrenaline.

At work, I took on more responsibilities. I was not only serving my clients and leading my team, I was put in charge of managing an office full of other financial advisors. I chose not to view this new responsibility as more work; it was going to be a way to further test and expand my Truest Fans skills. The folks who worked with me would get more than a boss; they would have a Truest Fan. And hopefully, by rooting them on, they would spread the Truest Fan gospel.

At church, I tried to take my leadership responsibilities more seriously. Instead of just doing what was required, I volunteered to lead a major fundraising campaign. Again, I didn't think about it as work. After all, no person in

> Each new day was like an adventure. I felt energized and ready to meet it head on.

their right mind wants the job of asking other people for money. I decided it was a great chance to cheer on the entire congregation as we set ourselves a course for doing even more of God's work in the world.

Funny, I was doing more and accomplishing more in most every area of my life. But I wasn't feeling burdened or overwhelmed. The energy and enthusiasm that had come from diving headfirst into my Truest Fan calling was transformative.

I felt as if my life had changed forever.

At this point, I also found myself wondering if I was finished meeting new Truest Fan gurus. If my days of going to Indians' games with teachers of Truest Fans wisdom were done. I was certainly going to miss the excitement of this part of my journey if it was over.

Of course, that's exactly when Jack sent me to meet Willie. I was told to report to the hot dog stand under the left-field bleachers one hour before Friday night's big game. When I got there, I was simply supposed to ask for Willie.

*Strange*, I thought, *hot dogs*, recalling my recent experience in the luxury suite.

The early crowd on Friday night was huge. Everybody wanted the free bobblehead of Cleveland's all-time greatest third baseman who had recently been elected to the Hall of Fame in Cooperstown. My entrance pass to

> The energy and enthusiasm that had come from diving headfirst into my Truest Fan calling was transformative.

the game for that evening didn't entitle me to receive one. I was bummed and even more curious as to what would happen next.

When I showed up and asked for Willie, one of the concessionaires threw a yellow shirt at me and told me I was late. He not-so-politely asked me to get dressed. Figuring this must be part of the plan, I did as I was told.

A few minutes later, when I got back to the stand, I was greeted by a silver-haired gentleman with a wide-eyed grin who simply asked, "Are you ready to go to work, Brownie?"

"If you're Willie," I replied, "I'm all yours."

"That was easy," Willie remarked. "You're going to be easy to train." Over the next 10 minutes, he showed me how to use the cash register and serve hot dogs.

"I'll be right beside you," he assured. "It won't take long to get the hang of things. It's Dollar Dog Night. These folks love their one-dollar hot dogs."

And away we went, serving hot dog after hot dog. We didn't talk. In fact, we hardly had time to think.

One of the first things that surprised me was how many people waited in line, longer than they had to, to buy their food from Willie. I'd motion them to my register, and they'd tell me it was okay, they'd wait for Willie.

"I'm selling the same food," I'd say.

They'd answer, "Willie is our man."

A few times, when Willie's line got a little too long, he'd wink at a guest and motion them over to me. "Brownie is a good man; he'll take care of you," he'd say. Comforting them.

Next, I noticed how Willie never stopped smiling and always greeted each hot dog connoisseur like they were the only guest in the line. He'd offer comments and compliments that made each person feel special. Some even blushed. Even when they were going elbow-to-elbow with the stampede of anxious fans.

Willie was also quick to offer me and my fellow hot dog servers a hand. Problem with the cash register? Willie fixed it. Mixed up order? Willie straightened it out. Angry customer? Willie always knew the right words. He reminded me of an orchestra conductor, always squeezing out the right notes.

He reminded me of an orchestra conductor, always squeezing out the right notes.

Before I knew it, the national anthem was playing. Willie quickly stepped away from his post, took off his cap, motioned others to do the same and closed his eyes to listen. You could tell the anthem was important to him as he sang quietly along with reverence.

After caring for the crowd for another handful of minutes, Willie motioned me to follow him away from the hot dog stand. I was thankful for the break. Serving hot dogs to a big crowd of people was a lot tougher than it looked.

The next thing I knew we were climbing the bleacher stairs. Willie took me to the very top of the stadium to find our seats . . . in the nosebleed section.

"Perfect," he said. "A perfect night for baseball."

"You're right," I replied, hoping my time behind the hot dog counter was over.

"Brownie," he said, "you're all right. You can be on my team anytime you want."

"Thanks," I stammered, "but I don't think I'm cut out for that kind of work."

"Maybe not,'" he offered, "but isn't it good to know you could do it in a pinch?"

"Sure," I responded, "but I'm guessing there's more to this story."

Willie then asked me to tell him what I thought I learned.

People feel differently when they feel special. And they're quick to reply with kindness.

"Well, if I had to put it in a few words, I'd say smiles and compliments go a long way. People feel differently when they feel special. And they're quick to reply with kindness."

"Man, you hit the nail on the head," Willie said with his trademark smile. "Jack said you were a fast learner, and now I know that he was right."

"I was just watching how you handled yourself," I remarked. "Your smile was contagious. The way you treated the guests and the workers was masterful. You even had people asking to be served by you. You were like an artist at work. You really seemed to love what you were doing."

"I don't get to work the register very often anymore," he said. "It's one of the best jobs I ever had. Actually, it was the first real job I ever had. Sometimes I miss it."

"What do you do now?" I asked.

"I'm the head of concessions here at the stadium. I like to think of myself as the head chef to the most important diners in Cleveland. I mean, there's nothing more important than an Indians' game menu," he said, shrugging.

"So, with a big job like that, how could you find time to serve hot dogs for over an hour?" I wondered out loud.

"You wanted to learn the next Truest Fan lesson, didn't you?" he questioned back.

Sometimes you learn best by example.

"Yes."

"Well, that's why I worked the stand. Sometimes you learn best by example,"

Willie offered. "I wanted you to see Lesson #4 in action."

"Go on," I prodded.

"Lesson #4 of Truest Fan wisdom is *Smiles and kind words go a long way. When you're a Truest Fan, you're always on duty.*"

"That sounds like a tall order," I said. "Sounds like being a Truest Fan is a 24/7 endeavor."

"It is," Willie agreed. "But once you get the swing of things, it's almost automatic. Stop for a minute and think about the people you cross paths with when you're walking down the street. Do you notice how some people don't even look at you while some look at you with a frown?"

"I do," I replied. "Drives me crazy. Almost makes me feel like I'm trespassing."

"Have you ever tried to smile back with a simple hello?" he asked.

"Not very often," I said.

"What happens when you do?" Willie's interrogation continued.

"They're usually caught off guard, but then they offer back a faint smile and maybe even a quiet hello."

"Too many of us walk around on this planet with our heads down," Willie offered. "Like we're locked away in our own little worlds. But the truth is, we all need a little encouragement from our fellow human beings.

"A smile as you pass someone in the hall. A thank you from someone you help. An attaboy from someone who notices a small achievement. A word of encouragement from someone who notices that you may be feeling a bit down.

"None of these things costs us a nickel. And their return cannot be measured in dollars and cents. But their impact can be priceless.

"You never know when a smile, a wink, a nod, a hello or a word of encouragement touches someone's life in a way that lasts forever. And at the very least, those smiles and kind words have a compounding effect.

"Joy, happiness and love compound even faster than interest rates."

"You know, I see that all the time when I'm watching the Indians," I offered. "The guys are always picking each other up. A pat on the back, a thump of the mitt or an arm around the shoulder usually follows a blown play.

"The best players on our team lead by example. They're pumping the other guys up even when nobody's really paying attention to them. If, as a fan, you stop and watch what's happening away from the next pitch, you see it

We all need a little encouragement from our fellow human beings.

Joy, happiness and love compound even faster than interest rates.

catching on. They all play with an extra spring in their steps."

"Exactly," Willie affirmed. "Since I'm here all the time, I get to see it in practice. They don't just save it for game day. And every once in a while, I get to talk with some of the players and coaches. They talk about the importance of togetherness. They tell me they can't just fake it.

"Remember, players are coming and going all of the time. Sometimes a new guy comes in who is taking the spot of one of their best friends, and the leaders in the clubhouse make that guy feel welcome. After all, they all have the same goal.

"As fans, we do it too. We give the new guy the benefit of the doubt. Make them feel welcome. And it has an impact."

"Well, that's kind of easy since it's just a game, isn't it?" I wondered out loud.

"Maybe," Willie suggested, "but I like to think we can learn from the game. When we watch these guys come together year after year and win as many games as they have won even though we don't have a big player payroll, guys get hurt, trades get made and contracts expire, attitude matters. And when it's an attitude of each guy picking the next guy up, it's contagious. Even through the grind of a long season and all its ups and downs."

When it's an attitude of each guy picking the next guy up, it's contagious.

"You're right," I agreed. "Watching baseball, especially our Tribe . . . excuse the bias . . . is a great example for the way we should pick each other up.

"Every chance we get, we should look people in the eyes, smile and offer a word or gesture of encouragement. Doesn't cost anything, but it always makes the world a slightly better place."

"Right on," Willie acknowledged. "There's a great saying in the Old Testament: *Do justice, love kindness and walk humbly with God.* That was the first piece of advice I learned when I took my first job selling hot dogs for the Indians.

> Do justice, love kindness and walk humbly with God.

"I remember thinking how strange it was. I wondered what love, kindness and God had to do with asking people if they wanted ketchup or mustard. I just wanted to scratch out a living . . . pay my bills."

"Fortunately, the old guy who offered that advice didn't let it go. When he checked in on me, he always asked if I was walking the walk or just squawking the talk. Squawking was what we called the chatter we yelled as we were selling hot dogs in the stands.

"We'd say things like, 'Hey, get your hot dogs here. I got 'em with ketchup, I got 'em with relish. And I got 'em with good old-fashioned stadium mustard. Best hot dogs in all of the big leagues. Get you hot dogs here.'

"When he asked me that question, I'd always nod my head, say something stupid and try to avoid the conversation.

"And then, one day in the middle of the season, we heard that the old guy had had a heart attack. They weren't sure he was going to make it. We didn't know what to do. Most of us didn't even know his real name.

"A short time later, one of the fans in his section asked me what happened to the Hot Dog Man. I told him I was the hot dog man and asked him what he wanted. And that's when he told me I was just selling hot dogs, the old guy was THE Hot Dog Man.

"He had been serving this fan and most of the others in this section for almost three decades. He never missed a game. So, they were worried.

"When I told him about the heart attack, he was shocked. You would have thought I was talking about his best friend. The only thing he said to me was to come back in the seventh inning.

"Scratching my head, I went off to sell more hot dogs.

"When the seventh inning arrived, I found the man who had asked me to come back. He went on to tell me how important the Hot Dog Man had been to him and his friends. He told me he made the games better.

"His smiles, his kind words, his squawking and his talking had turned into a strange sort of friendship. Each season, the fans and the Hot Dog Man looked forward to spending time with each other. They were like a family.

"He said the Hot Dog Man had introduced most of their kids to Cleveland baseball. He had been to birthday parties, weddings and even funerals of fans who had sat in his section. They had even thrown him a party when they learned he had been working for the Indians for 25 years.

"To this fan, the Hot Dog Man was the epitome of someone who was walking a mighty fine walk. Loving others. Being kind. And walking humbly in God's footsteps.

"And that wasn't all.

"He handed me a huge pile of cash, told me he trusted me and asked me to make sure the Hot Dog Man got it. This crazy group of fans wanted to help with the Hot Dog Man's hospital bills. No questions asked.

"The next day, I found out from my boss exactly which hospital the Hot Dog Man was in. I went there to give him the cash. As I walked in the room, the look of surprise on

He was the epitome of someone who was walking a mighty fine walk. Loving others. Being kind. And walking humbly in God's footsteps.

his face caused me to worry. I didn't want to make him have another heart attack.

"When I explained why I was there, he was embarrassed. He told me he was going to be okay and he thought he'd be back at the stadium in a couple weeks. He asked me to give the money to the Indians' charitable foundation.

"When I asked him why, he simply said that he took care of those fans because that's what we're all supposed to do to the people we encounter in our lives. He said love, kindness and humility were his real purpose in life.

"I was blown away. And I told him I was ready to walk the walk. He told me he knew I'd do big things in my life and that all success comes from this one basic rule. The lesson he tried to teach me the first time I met him.

"Now, all these years later, I remember the Hot Dog Man every day. The stuff he taught me with that one nugget of wisdom has helped me accomplish big things and gotten me through more tough patches than I can remember.

"And that's why I think they're such an important part of Truest Fan wisdom."

"Now, that's quite a story," I said, "but I have to ask, where's the Hot Dog Man now?"

"Oh, that's easy," Willie motioned. "He's sitting right next to you. He's retired from the hot dog business."

As I glanced over, all I could see was a big fat smile as my newly discovered seatmate offered me a hand while saying, "I'm the Hot Dog Man, Brownie. Pleasure to make your acquaintance. I hope Willie hasn't talked your ear off. There's a baseball game going on, you know."

I could only smile back. Once again, this network of Truest Fans had blown me away. How could I learn so much from this crazy group of strangers? An odd collection of guys who were living amazing lives by walking the walk. Guys who were intentionally trying to help others.

> How could I learn so much from this crazy group of strangers?

"Enough of that," Willie broke in. "We've got a game to watch!"

Other than cheering on the Tribe and some friendly conversation, we didn't say much else to each other, but I knew I was where I was supposed to be.

As the game ended, Willie and the Hot Dog Man each gave me a firm embrace, told me they hoped to see me again soon and to be on the lookout for what was going to happen next.

"You'll love it," they both agreed.

"I'm sure I will," I said, mustering up my biggest smile. "Thanks for your love and kindness. You're a bigger blessing than you could possibly know."

You're a bigger blessing than you could possibly know.

Then, as if we had scripted it, we bumped fists and said with the reassurance of lifelong friends who were promising to see each other soon, "Truest Fans."

# MY PERSONAL ACTION PLAN

# LESSON #5

## Your family deserves your very best.

"Start children off on the way they should go, and even when they are old, they will not turn from it."

—Proverbs 22:6, NIV

"Love is the most important thing in the world, but baseball is pretty good, too."

—Yogi Berra (Yogi-ism), baseball great

The daily text messages I received from Willie over the next couple of weeks were one of a kind. Each time I read one I could see his smile in my mind's eye . . .

"Have you tried to make a new friend today?"

"Hey, hot dog man here, get your hot dog."

"A genuine smile goes a long way. Don't hide it."

"Have lunch at a table full of strangers and make them happy they met you."

"Let someone know how special they are today."

"Turn those frowns upside down."

"Pay it forward with a word of encouragement."

"Don't hide in the corner at the coffee shop, make a new friend."

"You're still on duty, do your job the best you can."

"Go stand in a long line so you have to talk to people."

A genuine smile goes a long way. Don't hide it.

... and you could tell he was thinking about all the opportunities that come about every day to make other people feel better about themselves. Or simply add a little joy to their days.

What could be wrong with that?

At first, since I sometimes avoided eye contact as I went about my day, it was really, really hard. I couldn't wait for the other person to acknowledge me; I had to take the first step.

I turned it into a game. I started each day with five pennies in my left pocket. Every time I made a stranger smile or paid a compliment to someone I barely knew, I moved a penny to my right pocket. And then I reversed the direction. I wanted to end each with all five pennies back in my left pocket.

At first, it was hard. I had to keep my eyes wide open when I wandered around the office or walked down the street. On days when I was glued to my desk chair, I had to go out of my way to find a place or two to where I'd run into a live human being. After about a week, I got the hang of it, so instead of just trying to have my pennies make a round trip through my pants pockets, I tried to see if I could make each day a personal record.

Sounds strange, but it was fun. I even extended my efforts into meetings and phone calls. I tried to say something extra positive to each person who sat around the table in my meetings. And I tried to see if I could get receptionists and secretaries who answered my call to laugh at something silly I would say.

It was crazy, but the more I tried to surprise others, the more relaxed I felt. The compliments, praises and goofy smiles had a boomerang effect; I was happier. The more I tried to be a Truest Fan to complete strangers, the friendlier everyone around me became.

This was after just a few weeks. I wondered how it might compound over time.

After a few weeks of the penny game, my texts from Willie were interrupted by a message from an unnamed person who asked me to meet for coffee. I was assured that this meet-up would be another step in my Truest Fan journey.

Of course, I quickly accepted. This Truest Fan journey had become a healthy addiction.

When I arrived for coffee, I was greeted by a woman named Sue. As we began to talk, I found that she had an unassuming personality. She seemed quiet, maybe even a bit shy. But you could immediately tell she possessed something special and she wanted to share it.

As we settled into our conversation, she asked me if I remembered Bruiser.

"Absolutely," I said. "He's the one who got me started on my Truest Fan adventure."

> The more I tried to be a Truest Fan to complete strangers, the friendlier everyone around me became.

"Well," she replied, "he's my husband."

"Wow," I responded. "No offense, but I wouldn't have put the two of you together in a million years."

"I get that all the time," she remarked. "We are quite an odd couple.'

"How did you meet?" I asked.

"Well, believe it or not, kind of the same way you did. At an Indians' game. He tried to catch a foul ball and it ended up bouncing up and hitting him in the chin. The ushers brought him back to my first aid station to bandage up a small cut."

"That's funny," I said. "A tough guy like that can't even handle a foul ball."

"He's a bit of a dork," she explained. "He's always experiencing little mishaps. That's one of the things that makes him so lovable."

"He's made a huge difference in my life," I said, "and I only spent a few hours with him."

At that point, Sue wanted to get down to business. She explained that she was a woman of few words, but she felt she had an important role to play in helping others become Truest Fans.

"Besides," she quipped, "not everyone needs three hours at an Indians' game to spread the good word."

I decided not to argue.

Sue went on to tell me how her Truest Fan attitude had actually made her a better nurse. In addition to working part-time for the Indians, she was a registered nurse in the intensive care unit at a nearby hospital. She talked about the way she had become almost callous when treating patients and speaking with their loved ones.

"Like they were cars on the assembly line at the Ford plant."

And when Bruiser began to share his Truest Fan experience with her, she decided to follow his lead. She wanted to become a Truest Fan nurse.

"I don't have any way of proving it," she said, "but our patient success seemed to improve. There were a lot fewer sad faces in the waiting rooms. And our staff, even the doctors, all seemed to work better together. My work as a nurse became a joy again."

> My work as a nurse became a joy again.

"But that's not what I want to talk about," she said. "I have a totally different lesson to share with you."

"Okay," I agreed, "but what could be more important?"

"Not more important," she said, "just another critical part of becoming a Truest Fan."

"You see, I became a better wife, Bruiser became a better husband and we both became a better couple because of our Truest Fan journeys. Sometimes when you're off doing important things, it's easy to take your spouse for granted. You think they're along for the ride, but they don't necessarily know where they're going."

"I think I know what you mean," I commented. "I know my wife has recognized a change in me, but I haven't fully shared everything I've been learning."

"Typical husband," she joked.

I just nodded my head as if I understood.

You need to be a Truest Fan of your wife and your family. They deserve the best of everything you're doing for yourself and for others.

"Well," she went on, "you need to be a Truest Fan of your wife and your family. They deserve the best of everything you're doing for yourself and for others. Plus, since you go home to them every night, you have time to talk about it."

"I get it," I agreed, "but I guess we're like a lot of folks; we get so caught up in our routines, like running our girls around to all their events, that we don't always find time to talk about what's really going on in our lives. I think I've been screwing up."

"Forget it," she encouraged. "There's no better time to start than today."

"How do I get started?" I asked.

"Not to overstate the obvious," she replied, "but you just need to share what you're learning with your wife and daughters. I bet you have some great stories to tell. Not just the stories of your meetings with your Truest Fan mentors, but the opportunities you're having each day to share what you've learned."

"You're exactly right," I said. "In fact, if I shared everything, I bet we'd be up late into the night. There's no shortage of material."

"I don't like to admit this," she said softly, "but while Bruiser was learning his first Truest Fan lessons, I was looking for a divorce attorney. I thought our marriage was over. I saw how Bruiser's success was actually causing him to be unhappy and that was spilling over on me and our kids. Each evening, when the family was together, we were all walking on eggshells.

"So, when Bruiser saw the Truest Fan light, I was actually pissed. I wondered how he could be so happy while I was increasingly miserable. I even wondered if it was another woman.

"And then one morning, I saw him sending out a bunch of text messages and I decided to confront him. I asked him to show me his phone. He didn't hesitate. When I saw all the messages to people I didn't even know, I asked him to explain.

> You just need to share what you're learning with your wife and daughters. I bet you have some great stories to tell.

"He told me that he had become a Truest Fan and his job every morning was to make people smile. Let them know they were loved and that someone was thinking about them.

"Of course, that wasn't what I was expecting. I started to cry.

"When he asked me what was wrong, I told him I was jealous. How he could share that much love with so many other people and not share it with me and our children?

"Like the big dummy he is, he wondered what I was talking about. He went on to say he has always been our Truest Fan even if he hadn't called it that before. He believed he was rooting for all of us each and every day. In fact, he felt the relationships he had at home were the only things that were going really well while he was commiserating in his personal and professional funk.

"That's when I told him about the divorce attorney. He was stunned. He began to cry like a little baby.

"Bruiser immediately called off all of his appointments for that day. We spent the entire day together having some of the most important conversations we've ever had before.

"We were both stunned by how much we had drifted apart without knowing that we had drifted apart. Bruiser admitted to ignoring the distance that has come between us by staying busy in his work. At the same time, I was unable to ignore it, but I held it in and didn't share my thoughts with him. We were both on the same page, but we didn't know it, and it was the wrong page to be on.

"Bruiser quickly saw how the changes he was making away from our home were almost in isolation of what was going on at home. He said that if I were him, I would be upset too.

"We spoke about our children. We wondered how our lack of communication was showing up in their lives. Of course, we believed they were happy, and they were, but they weren't seeing us acting at our best.

"And we knew that had to change.

"As we were talking, we both recalled a passage from Proverbs: *Start children off on the way they should go, and even when they are old, they will not turn from it.*

> Start children off on the way they should go, and even when they are old, they will not turn from it.

"We both agreed that that was a legacy worth building.

"We remarked that we had been lucky. We'd done more right than wrong, so we shouldn't beat each other up. But we needed to do more. And like most of the Truest Fan wisdom we had shared with each other we marveled that there was no better time to start or, maybe in our case, to pick up the pieces than right then.

"I asked him, 'Are you in?'

"'Absolutely,' he replied without hesitation.

"And then, like we had said it a million times, we exclaimed in unison, 'We're in this together!'"

"What a great testimony, Sue," I chimed in. "So much of what you said sounds exactly like my wife and me right now."

"I know," she offered, clearly trying not to sound arrogant. "So many of us have been right where you and your family are. Hovering between getting by and true happiness. I often wonder why it's so tough to push ourselves over the edge."

"True that," I said, "but I feel like there's more to learn from your experience. What happened next?"

We committed to intentional family time.

"We committed to intentional family time," she answered. "We started by agreeing that we would have an 'executive' meeting each and every week, an hour where the two of us would talk about our progress in the past week, make plans for the new week and reaffirm our marriage vows."

She turned red.

"Why are you blushing?" I asked.

"Well," she said, "some of our executive sessions have turned into some of the best sex we have ever had."

"Whoa, too much information," I reacted.

"Sorry," she said, "that's the most embarrassing part of sharing this Truest Fan lesson. But you deserve full disclosure. It's one of the many perks of becoming a Truest Fan.

"Enough said," she chirped, "so let me finish.

"In addition to our executive sessions, we also committed to a minimum of three family times each week. Sometimes it was family dinners. Although, with our schedules and the kids' schedules, that was much harder than it sounded. But we knew each week would give us the time we needed if we simply planned ahead. That's why it became a top agenda item for our executive sessions.

> We knew each week would give us the time we needed if we simply planned ahead.

"And the cool thing was, our kids initially pushed back. They told us it sounded like we were going through some sort of old age crisis. But it didn't matter. They were kind of right. And we committed to easing into things. Fortunately, that didn't take long.

"Once our kids got engaged, they were all-in. Sometimes they would even call for impromptu family meetings so they could share good news, talk about something that was bugging them or discuss an unusual situation they had run into where they might value our point of view. They thought they were learning something. Bruiser and I learned so much more. Especially the value of being each other's Truest Fans.

"We saved our marriage. But, more importantly, we learned how to be a family. Week in and week out. Day after day after day."

"Amazing," I said. "So simple, but so profound."

"There's one more thing," Sue jumped in. "We also planned an epic vacation. And it was NOT a budget-busting vacation for the rich and famous. We simply committed to two weeks away in a very inexpensive cabin in the mountains. We made sure there was plenty of stuff to do. We all tend to get bored too easily. We looked for things like hiking trails, famous sites we could visit on day trips and places we could splash in the water. Best vacation ever.

"Funny thing though . . . after a couple of days of staying 'busy,' we spent most of the last ten days just hanging out by the cabin . . . enjoying each other's company. It was like we realized that the greatest vacation is sometimes just the time you spend with your family."

"You lost me at two weeks," I replied. "That seems like a long, long time to be away from the real world. Sometimes one week is hard to squeeze in. Long weekends seem like a luxury."

"We thought that too," Sue said. "Truth is, it isn't enough. We all have busy lives and we can't always afford the time to get away. But the most important thing we learned is that time with family is fleeting.

"The older our kids get, the less time they have too. So, no matter what, we plan for at least one epic adventure every year. Some years we've been able to have more than one. Some years two weeks has turned into three or four. And some years, we've had to plan our epic adventures at home.

"The biggest trick is to build epic family adventures into your life. You'll never regret it."

"Let me make sure I have this right," I offered. "You have three secrets for making Truest Fan Lesson #5 come alive in your lives:

1.  Weekly executive sessions with fringe benefits
2.  At least 3 family meetings each week.
3.  And take at least 1 epic adventure each year.

"Did I get that right?"

"Yes," she smiled, "exactly right. But never make it feel like a sacrifice or hard work or an off-putting set of rules. Think of it as a launching point. A barometer. A way to get the ball rolling. You'll end up finding that it's part of the rhythm of your life. And if you ever wander off course, those three secrets are like a north star; they will put you back on track."

> The biggest trick is to build epic family adventures into your life. You'll never regret it.

"So cool," I offered, "but aren't your kids grown and on their own now?"

"Yes, they are," she answered quickly, "but that hasn't caused us to quit. We still have our executive sessions and they include conversations about our kids' spouses and our newborn granddaughter and the grandchildren we hope will come soon. Since our kids are in different parts of the world, we can't always meet three times per week, but rarely a week goes by when we don't all get on a call or a video chat together. And, every year, we book two weeks at a nice getaway and invite them all to join us for as little or as much time as they can. The time together is so special because it also includes our growing family."

"Wow, you've created traditions," I said.

> Truest Fan wisdom is like the missing pieces from a big puzzle. Once you find the pieces, it is obvious where they need to go.

"Exactly right," Sue responded. "Our almost-too-late epiphany on being Truest Fans to each other has turned into a legacy that we hope lasts for generations to come."

At that point, Sue excused herself and I was left wondering, *Truest Fan wisdom is like the missing pieces from a big puzzle. Once you find the pieces, it is obvious where they need to go.*

I couldn't wait to get home and start sharing what I had been learning. I was certain that Bruiser, Ken, Willie and Sue would mean as much to my bride as they did to me.

# MY PERSONAL ACTION PLAN

# LESSON #6

## You are never alone. God is your Truest Fan.

"God made you so he could love you."

—Rick Warren, pastor

"Be strong and courageous; do not be frightened or dismayed, for the Lord your God is with you wherever you go."

—Joshua 1:9, NRSV

"I've come to the conclusion that the two most important things in life are good friends and a good bullpen."

—Bob Lemon, Cleveland Indians legend

N ow, I bet you're expecting another story like the last few. And I wish I could tell you that my next Truest Fan adventure followed that same happy pattern.

It didn't.

Yes, I received daily texts from Sue. She became a cheerleader for me, my wife and our girls.

"Family time is prime time."

"Plan for the epic."

"Did you make it to the play?"

"Hug the ones you love."

"When it comes to family, there's no time like the present."

"How's the sex?"

And yes, I had begun to share my Truest Fan stories with my wife, Lori. She had quickly become as eager to learn about them as I had. We hadn't stayed up so many nights past midnight, just talking, since we had first fallen in love.

Lori could now see why the changes she had mentioned she was noticing in me were so

When it comes to family, there's no time like the present.

palpable. How they had encircled so many parts of our lives.

She felt like she had changed, even though she didn't know exactly how or why. She was certain our girls were happier because of the calm, peace and love that was growing in our family each day.

Even though I hadn't previously shared the lessons I was learning.

During one of our late-night talks she said, "Wow, this is powerful. I'm now just beginning to learn the actual lessons, but I can see that the energy that comes from being around Truest Fans is contagious."

> The energy that comes from being around Truest Fans is contagious.

I couldn't have said it any better myself.

Still, tragedy struck. My wife, Lori, was diagnosed with breast cancer. The same disease that had taken my mother. The same cancer that had kept my mother from ever getting to know her grandchildren on this earth. I was numb.

Why had I waited so long to tell her how much I loved her? I worried that my Truest Fan stories and all I had learned from my new friends had come too late. Would she just see the things I was trying to do now as my way of caring for her while she was going through seemingly endless doctors' appointments, treatments, surgery and prescriptions? When I told her how beautiful she was would she think I was just being nice because she bore the scar of a missing breast?

Even now, as I write these words, I discover that my worry about what Lori would think about the way I was treating her was really more my feeling sorry for myself. I had had a pretty damn good life. No real tragedies. A family who loved me. A good career. In all, not really a care in the world.

Was I more worried about the interruption to my life or the battle Lori was facing? Was this Truest Fan stuff just a nice philosophy to make people feel good about themselves? I questioned everything.

Then, one evening about 60 days into her cancer journey, Lori grabbed me by the hand and told me she was my Truest Fan and that it was in large part because she knew, even though things weren't going as planned, I was her Truest Fan. She talked about the stories I had been telling her about my Truest Fan journey: The people I had met and the lessons they had taught me. The way she was seeing me transform before her eyes.

I thought I was failing. Lori saw the opposite.

I didn't think I was sharing and caring enough, but she told me how sometimes she pretended to be asleep and basked in the warmth of me holding her hand and talking to myself. Talking to myself and telling her what I was

I thought I was failing. Lori saw the opposite.

learning as I tried to even better understand my purpose as a Truest Fan.

She said I was her hero. When I knew, deep down, she was the real hero. Her bravery, strength and perseverance through her battle with cancer were amazing. The love she gave to our daughters, her caregivers and anyone who visited her far surpassed anything we were trying to share with her.

She told me that she didn't plan to lose her battle with cancer, but the renewed love our family had developed for each other gave her the confidence to know we would be okay if she were to die. If we could be each other's Truest Fans through this horrible time in our lives, we could keep on doing it no matter what life threw our way.

> If we could be each other's Truest Fans through this horrible time in our lives, we could keep on doing it no matter what life threw our way.

"Don't give up," she encouraged and drifted off to sleep.

My mind was racing. How could she be so wise? How could she know so much about what I was learning about being a Truest Fan? How could she show such remarkable love when she was the one facing life-and-death circumstances?

How could I be so selfish?

And, for the first time, I had to actually ponder Lori's death. To that point, I had been in denial. My actions may have meant more to Lori and our girls than I had thought they did, but, at least in my mind, I had been operating in a fog.

*What should a Truest Fan do now?* I asked myself.

I did not sleep easily that night.

The next morning, as if on cue, I received a series of messages . . .

> From Bruiser: *Time for a full court press.*
>
> From Bruiser: *Root for yourself.*
>
> From Ken: *You have important work to do.*
>
> From Jack: *It's how you play the game.*
>
> From Willie: *Smiles and kind words, my friend, smiles and kind words.*
>
> From Sue: *Family is worth the fight.*
>
> Finally: *My name is John-Patrick. You're ready for your final Truest Fan lesson. I'll meet you for lunch at the Indians' game today.*

Smiles and kind words, my friend, smiles and kind words.

When I checked my email a couple minutes later, I found an electronic ticket with a note containing instructions telling me I would find John-Patrick in the Terrace Club, the big windowed restaurant overlooking left field. Just ask for him at the front desk. And after we had lunch, we would go down to our seats.

*That's crazy*, I thought. *With everything going on in my life right now, I don't have time for a baseball game. Especially in the middle of the workday. I hardly have enough time for my business.*

And then, five more messages hit my inbox, one from each Truest Fan mentors. Each with the exact same message: *Just do it!*

The very next minute, Lori walked into the den and asked, "Are you going to the Indians' game today? I know how much you love a businessman's special (a weekday, day game) at the stadium. It's going to be a gorgeous day."

"Whoa," I said. "Who put you up to that?"

"No one," she answered. "I think you deserve a break. Just do it."

*Spooky*, I thought and quickly made plans to meet John-Patrick.

I arrived at the stadium restaurant right on time and the hostess led me to my table, saying John-Patrick was already waiting.

"You're in for a treat," she further commented. "He's one of the most fascinating men I've ever met. He makes everyone feel special."

"No doubt," I replied. "I've met some of his friends and they are all very special people too."

"I've met them," she said with a wry smile on her face as if she knew something I didn't know.

But I didn't have time to think about that further. We had reached the table with the best view of the field in the restaurant and the hostess said, "John-Patrick, here's your lunch guest. Enjoy the game."

As John-Patrick thanked her, he got up from his seat, swallowed me in a bear hug like we had been best friends forever and let me know how excited he was to have a new friend with whom he could enjoy some Tribe baseball.

As I began to thank him for the invitation, I noticed what a huge man he was and that he was dressed in a black, three-piece suit with a black dress shirt and a starched white collar.

He noticed my stare.

"I couldn't get by the rectory before coming over to the game," he said.

"Tell you what," he continued, "let's take off our neckwear and get a bit more comfortable."

He removed his white collar and stuck it in his pocket. I did the same with my tie. I had come straight to the game from my office.

"Rectory?" I questioned,

"Oh yeah," he answered, "I'm the head pastor over at Our Lady of Angels. I was visiting with a parishioner this morning and planned to stop by the rectory to put on something less formal but ran out of time. Since I can't attend day games on Sunday, I try to never miss a businessman's special."

"Wow," I said. "This isn't what I was expecting."

"Yup," he shot back, "the Truest Fan crew is a motley group. I'm just glad they let me in the club. We religious types can cause trouble."

"That's not what I meant," I said, somewhat defensively. "But, in truth, I shouldn't have expected anything. Everyone I've met on this journey has been very different. Except when it comes to being a Truest Fan."

"All colors, shapes and sizes, Brownie," he agreed. "All colors, shapes and sizes."

After the waiter took our order, JP, as he told me he preferred to be called, said the plan was to have a nice talk over lunch and then move down to our seats around the third inning. He was excited about our tickets, box seats in the shade, right behind the Indians' on-deck circle.

"Best seats in the house," he chuckled. "Courtesy of one of my parishioners. One of the perks of the job.

"Now, Brownie," JP went on, "tell me, how Lori is doing? I hear she got some bad news from the doctors a couple months back."

"How did you hear that?" I asked, totally surprised by this question from a man I had never met before.

"Truest Fans have a way of keeping up with each other, Brownie. You should know that by now. We keep an eye out for each other."

"But I haven't said a word to any of them," I countered. "How could they know?"

"Well," he replied, "Willie bumped into one of your coworkers at last night's game. You had introduced them a couple months ago. They got talking and your name came up. And now we're having lunch."

"Small world," I sighed. "I kept this news pretty bottled up."

"Yeah," JP offered back. "Bad news has a way of swallowing you whole. Before you know it, it takes on a life of its own."

> Bad news has a way of swallowing you whole. Before you know it, it takes on a life of its own.

"Tell me about it," I confessed. "It wasn't until last night when Lori and I had a heart-to-heart conversation that I began to understand how much I had made her cancer all about me. I felt so horrible. Fortunately, she's a great lady and she let me know I wasn't doing as bad of a job as I had thought. And she's certainly glad I'm learning how to become a Truest Fan."

"It can be like a batting slump in baseball," JP offered. "The longer it lasts, the more you try to put the fate of the whole team on your shoulders. You take no satisfaction when the team wins, and you blame yourself for the losses.

"You start talking to yourself in the batter's box. All while everything the coaches suggest goes in one ear and out the other. You take encouragement from your teammates as if they're just feeling sorry for you. You sit at the end of the bench all by yourself because you don't want your bad luck to rub off on anybody else. It's a vicious cycle.

"And then, once you start putting a few hits together, you realize what an absolute jerk you've been. You mend your ways and feel like you're a part of the team again."

"Thanks," I said, "that makes perfect sense."

"I knew it would," JP said assuredly. "You've been a pretty quick study from everything that I've heard."

When you play like a team, rooting each other on, the journey is more than worth all the struggles. Every player is stronger for the effort.

"Life is a lot like a baseball team," I suggested. "You have winning streaks and losing streaks. Good years and bad years. But when you play like a team, rooting each other on, the journey is more than worth all the struggles. Every player is stronger for the effort."

"Preach it, Brownie," JP joked. "Sounds like the topic for a good sermon.

"And speaking of sermons, do you mind if I dig a little bit deeper with you?"

"I think I can handle it," I replied cautiously. "I've learned an awful lot hanging out at Tribe games with Truest Fans."

"Me too," he said.

"Yet, sometimes we isolate ourselves. Even when we're surrounded by lots of people. People who love us and want what's best for us.

"It's like we have a sign floating over our heads that says, 'don't even look at me, just leave me alone.'

"But here's the thing . . . it's impossible to be alone.

"Sure . . . it's possible to feel lonely. But there is a huge difference between feeling lonely and actually being alone.

> It's possible to feel lonely. But there is a huge difference between feeling lonely and actually being alone.

"Because there is someone looking over our shoulders every minute of every day. He knows what we think, what we want and all those thoughts and dreams we have buried deeply (and not so deeply) in our hearts and in our minds.

"He doesn't want to be a pest or an annoyance. He doesn't want you to feel like big brother is watching. He's not waiting for you to get tripped up so he can tell you, 'I told you so.'

"But he's there, nonetheless. Omnipresent in all of his glory. Standing ready to hug you, hold your hand and walk right beside you. His greatest hope is that you allow him in.

"He is the Truest Fan you will ever know.

"And turning to him can be done in an instant. There isn't a litmus test. There isn't a secret code. There isn't a waiting room. You just need to ask him to come sit beside you. You don't have to shout. Although you could. You don't have to say please. Although it may help. You can feel grief, despair and anger and he'll still listen. He doesn't have a thin skin.

"Most important, you just have to come to him with a willingness to accept his abiding love and friendship. To lay your thoughts and desires in his hands. And to let him root you on as quietly or as loudly as you like.

He wants you to know he's got your back.

"He wants you to know he's got your back."

"Don't get me wrong; it's not always easy. Sometimes as much as we know we have someone on our side, ready to root us on, we miss all the signals. And this may especially be true when it comes to asking God for his support. After all, it's not the same as picking up your phone and shooting off a quick text."

I was stunned. JP was pouring it on thick and I couldn't get enough.

"I believe in God," I said, "and we go to church most Sundays, but I never thought about him that way before. I tend to shut him out. Especially when it feels like I'm asking for his help.

"Is there a Truest Fan lesson in there somewhere?"

"Yes, there is, Brownie," JP responded. "What do you think it is?"

"You're never alone. God is your Truest Fan," I offered.

"Grand slam," JP shouted, and he wasn't talking about my answer.

You're never alone. God is your Truest Fan.

I had completely forgotten the fact that we were at a baseball game. And just as I had offered my suggestion, Cleveland's hottest hitter had just hit a grand slam home run to help us take back the lead.

"Sorry," JP said apologetically, "I caught that fly ball out of the corner of my eye and I could not help but let out a cheer."

"Your answer was a grand slam too. Congratulations, you understand the first six lessons of Truest Fans wisdom. There's one more."

*Great*, I thought, secretly hoping these lessons would never end.

"Thanks," I said out loud. "It's hard to believe there could be more. Learning to lean on God, even when you feel like your circumstances will never improve, seems like a lesson that could never be topped."

"In a way you're right," JP acknowledged, "but remember, even though each one of the Truest Fans lessons is valuable on its own, they are much, much more powerful together.

"But, for a few more minutes, let's keep focusing on God's presence in our lives," he continued. "Even when you're going through things like your wife having cancer and wondering how you and your daughters could ever live without her.

"God is there to answer your toughest questions.

"You can yell at him when you're angry.

"He'll be there to celebrate with you if there's a cancer-free proclamation.

"Or to console you if things go terribly wrong.

"He's your Truest Fan through thick and thin. And just like the rest of us, all he really asks is that you do your best to be his Truest Fan too."

"Thanks," I said. "I know the next few months won't be easy. And I may sometimes forget what you taught me. But I'll do my best to never forget that I am not alone."

"Good on you, Brownie. I know you'll do great. And I'll hold you, your wife and you family deeply in my prayers." JP began to get up.

"But for the next couple hours, let's go watch some Tribe baseball.

"Plus, I have a surprise for you."

## MY PERSONAL ACTION PLAN

# LESSON #7

## Intentionally live the life you were intended to live.

"Go and do likewise."

—Luke 10:37, NIV

"A life is not important except in the impact it has on other lives."

—Jackie Robinson, baseball legend

JP and I left the Terrace Club for our seats in the middle of the third inning. As we walked down the steps to our section, I saw a growing number of people staring at the jumbotron, the giant video screen above the outfield bleachers, cheering and clapping their hands.

When I turned and looked at the giant screen, I saw a picture of Lori with these words underneath: *We're your Truest Fans, Lori. Stay strong. We're rooting for you.*

With tears running down my cheeks, I could hear the crowd getting louder and louder. They were giving Lori a standing ovation. She might not have been there to see it or hear it, but the energy they were sending her way was electric.

I felt the power of Truest Fans from thousands of people I didn't even know.

As most everyone took their seats and we continued toward our row, I saw five people still standing and clapping and shouting my name, "Brownie, Brownie, Brownie . . ."

Bruiser, Ken, Jack, Willie and Sue were cheering for me.

I felt the power of Truest Fans from thousands of people I didn't even know.

I burst out in laughter.

Entering our row, JP and I were greeted with high fives, fist bumps and hugs. The stadium felt like home.

Sitting down, JP told me I should treat the rest of the game like a graduation ceremony. Each member of my Truest Fan faculty had something they wanted to share.

At that point, Sue was sitting next me, and she grabbed hold of my arm. She suggested we just watch a little baseball, let things settle in and then she would have something she wanted to tell me. After the exhilaration of the procession to our seats, that felt like the exact right thing to do. It ended up being one of those innings that took longer than it should but nothing really exciting happened. Watching the game like that is kind of like watching the waves roll in at the ocean on a calm day. You just take it in without any grand expectations. You're just glad you're there to enjoy the beauty of the game.

Sue broke the calm by saying, "I was so sad to learn about Lori's illness. You two were getting ready to do some really great things. And then you hit a brick wall."

"The timing was awful. But, then again, bad news never really has good timing."

"As I thought about the way you must feel, I could only think how even more important it is to give your family your best. . . while at the same time any feelings of hopelessness may make you doubt that your best is really your best."

"Just remember to try. You'll hit the mark more often than you think. If you have a bad day, don't beat yourself up. Tomorrow is another day."

"And the small victories you will have will compound. You, Lori and your girls will come out stronger in the end."

"Trust in the Truest Fan wisdom to be each other's biggest cheerleaders."

With that, she got up and Willie took her seat. As she looked back at me, she held her finger over her lips. She didn't even need a thank you.

*What grace*, I thought.

Willie quickly slapped me on the back and pointed to the pitcher's mound. "Here come three strikeouts in a row," he predicted. "Our guy has these hitters second guessing them-selves on every pitch."

We started calling balls and strikes together. In no time, Willie's prediction came true. And on the last strike of the inning, everybody in our row yelled "strike three" in unison.

They could probably hear us in Cincinnati . . . we were playing the Reds that day.

Trust in the Truest Fan wisdom to be each other's biggest cheerleaders.

As things quieted down, Willie asked me if I was still smiling and sharing kind words.

"As often as I can," I replied. "Some days have been tougher than others."

"That's what I wanted to hear, Brownie," he responded. "Some days you have to plaster on that smile with a little extra lipstick. Some days the words don't flow so smoothly. So, you just give it your best and let the chips fall where they may."

"Lori's been dealt a bad hand, but your love, warmth and encouragement will always be her best medicine."

"And I'll bet you see some of that in return. It's the boomerang effect of being a Truest Fan."

"You're right," I said. "Just last evening, Lori made me feel like a million bucks and I was the one who was trying to boost her spirits."

> The more you give, the more you get. Even when you least expect it.

"The more you give, my man, the more you get. Even when you least expect it," he said.

"Let me see a big smile."

I shot back my biggest, toothy grin. We both laughed loudly.

And then Jack took Willie's seat.

"This is amazing, Jack," I said, shaking his hand. "I'm not going to even try to guess how you all pulled this off."

"Truest Fans do crazy things sometimes, Brownie," Jack replied. "It's how we roll."

"Come on, Jack," I ribbed. "You all aren't that cool."

"You're right," he quickly returned, "but sometimes when you're playing the game the way it was meant to be played, you look like all-stars even if you're the bad news bears."

"Touché, Jack, touché."

"Brownie, you're finding out that the game isn't always fair. A new set of rules is being thrown at you. You have no control over them, but you still have to give it your utmost."

"And as you know from my story, when you give it your best, you can still expect some good to happen. You just have to keep playing."

> The only way you really lose is to give up.

"The only way you really lose is to give up."

"Never, never ever give up."

"Play as hard as you can until the last out."

Just then, the Tribe's first baseman yelled to us from the on-deck circle, "Hey Jack, Hey Brownie, great to see you guys. Thanks for all you're doing down at the children's home. My spies are sending me good reports."

Jack and I looked at each other with an "oh no we shouldn't" look and then shouted in unison, "How about a home run for the kids?"

Our hometown hero didn't look back. He stepped straight to the plate and nodded at the pitcher. Boom! The crack of the bat silenced the crowd. We all witnessed one of the most majestic home runs we have ever seen.

The stadium erupted in thunderous applause. Fireworks crackled from beyond the bleacher seats. And our guy nonchalantly trotted around the bases. As he passed home plate, he looked our way and simply gave us a thumbs-up.

Jack and I looked into each other's eyes and said in tandem, "It's how you play the game."

There was nothing else to say.

Jack then motioned Ken to take his seat as my commencement exercises continued. As Ken sat down, he quickly said, "You have important work to do. Don't delay."

"I get it, Ken," I responded, "but you sound so serious."

"Important work is serious, Brownie," Ken continues, "and sometimes it's not exactly what you thought it might be."

"Tell me about it. My important work has almost turned my life completely upside down since the last time we talked. I've had to put a new, never-wanted, never-expected job at the very top of my wall."

"And that's when you know you really get Lesson #3," he said. "When you can take something down from your wall for even more important work."

"As sad as I am for what's happening, I'm proud of you, Brownie. And I'm confident that you and your family will work through all of this; you'll end up exactly where you need to be. You simply need to continue to have faith in the process."

"And I think you do. I can see it in your eyes."

"Yes, I absolutely do," I said. "And if I ever had any doubts, they've been eliminated by the way you all have taught me each of the Truest Fan lessons."

"You all walk the walk and talk the talk," I continued.

"Until yesterday, you had no idea what was going on with my wife and within less than 24 hours, you introduced me to John-Patrick and my final lesson. You get the whole stadium to cheer for Lori. And you all show up for my graduation exercise."

"Truest Fans in action to the infinite degree."

"Thanks, Brownie," Ken replied. "Just don't forget that for the teacher to teach, the student has to show up. Showing up is a big, big part of important work."

"Speaking of important work," Ken added, "it's time for Bruiser to take this seat."

"I don't know how much more I can take, Ken. I'm feeling pretty overwhelmed."

"Bear with us, Brownie. You'll be glad you did," Ken replied as he stepped away.

As Bruiser sat down, he put his huge arm over my shoulder, handed me a small box and told me to open it. When I looked inside, I found a coin that was about the same size as a fifty-cent piece. On the front, beneath the current day's date, it read, *Brownie, Truest Fan Graduate*. On the back was an abbreviated list of Truest Fan lessons:

1. Self
2. Important Work
3. Love
4. Smile
5. Family
6. God
7. Intentional

Then, as I looked up, everyone in my section held up their coins in a semi-salute. It wasn't just the six mentors who had led me through my Truest Fan graduation. There must have been over 100 people.

And as I glanced toward the field, several members of the Indians' team flashed their coins my way too. Including our home-run-hitting first baseman.

"Wow," I said to Bruiser, "Is this when we're supposed to throw our caps into the air?"

"You can if you want to," Bruiser replied, "but I think that would be taking things too far."

We grinned at each other in the knowledge that what was happening was pretty amazing. And that little else needed to be said or done.

"To tell you the truth, Brownie," Bruiser continued, "we've never pulled off such an extravagant graduation ceremony. Usually, it's just a handful of us getting together for a game or coffee and sharing a few words of wisdom."

"How about the coin?" I asked.

"That too," he said. "We believe it's important to have a reminder of our commitment to being Truest Fans in our pockets or hanging around our necks."

"So, what made my graduation so different?" I wondered out loud.

> Sometimes you have to shake things up to make sure the message doesn't get drowned out by life's distractions.

"The circumstances," he answered. "Sometimes being Truest Fans requires a little extra celebration. Sometimes you have to shake things up to make sure the message doesn't get drowned out by life's distractions."

"My family and I have had a big distraction for sure—" I admitted.

"That's putting it mildly," Bruiser interrupted. "And it seems to me you're already seeing the light on the other side of the tunnel. We just wanted to make sure."

"Kind of like shaking up the batting order when the team is on a losing stretch," I thought out loud. "You're still the same team. Rooting for each other. But you have to be willing to accept a different role."

"Good way to put it," Bruiser said in agreement.

"What's next?" I asked, not needing anything else, but also not wanting to be surprised.

"Just do it!" Bruiser exclaimed. "Intentionally live the life you were intended to live."

Something didn't register. JP had told me there was going to be a seventh lesson. And the back of the coin contained the word "Intentional" next the number seven.

"Wait a second," I said as I looked at the coin again, "that's the seventh Truest Fan lesson, isn't it?"

"Yes, it is," Bruiser said matter-of-factly. "It's the lesson that reminds each of us not to take our cause for granted. Without intentionality, we run the risk of letting our lessons just become another set of well-meaning ideas that don't make a real difference in the world."

"That's a bold claim," I stated.

"This is an important cause," he urged. "There is no limit to the good we can do if we constantly remember to do the things we say we are going to do. If we turn our words, lessons and wisdom into action."

As the game continued, I couldn't help but think that this was one of the best days of my life and that it didn't have to end.

It was up to me and my Truest Fan tribe to keep the momentum going.

> There is no limit to the good we can do if we constantly remember to do the things we say we are going to do.

## MY PERSONAL ACTION PLAN

# EPILOGUE

A few months later, a package arrived in the mail. The return address only read, *Truest Fans*, so I was anxious to rip it open.

As I tore off the outer packaging, a note dropped out:

> *Brownie,*
>
> *Only open this the rest of the way if you're with Lori. We'll find out.*
>
> > *We love you,*
> > *Your Truest Fans*

Lori was out with our daughters and I didn't know when they'd be home, so this felt a little like torture. I'd been able to spend some time with my Truest Fan mentors since my graduation. Of course, we were always sending out our daily text messages. But none of them even hinted at another surprise.

The wait was going to drive me crazy.

So, as I sat on the couch in the family room, staring at the package, I decided to take stock of how I'd been doing. Had I been living up to my Truest Fan commitments?

Fortunately, I could quickly say yes.

That last lesson of intentionality was the glue that was helping me hold everything I had learned together. And for me, intentionality started with a new morning routine. I combined exercise with prayer and journaling.

Each morning, as I got out of bed, I'd pray, "God, please help me live an intentional life today. Please show me how to help others and make a difference in their lives. No matter how big or how small. I want to be an even better Truest Fan. Thank you for being my Truest Fan. Amen."

> I want to be an even better Truest Fan.

My short prayer was followed by a cardio routine to get my heart rate going, a cooling down time when I read scripture and meditated on the message, and then I journaled.

My journal was my tool for capturing ideas that I hoped would help me insert the Truest Fan lessons into every aspect of my life. Sometimes they focused on my family; other times they focused on my business; and still other times they were focused on my relationship with God.

No topic, no matter how crazy it may have felt at the time I was writing it, was off limits. And I felt certain my journaling was a big reason

Truest Fan wisdom guided me in so many of my everyday actions and decisions.

Most days, I even took a break in the middle of the day to reread some of what I had written. It was a chance to get recentered. Especially if I was having an extra busy or stressful day.

After all, being a Truest Fan didn't mean life would stop throwing craziness my way. I just wanted to be prepared to handle it the best I knew how. And I was getting better at it.

I could honestly say my Truest Fan commitment was continuing to be transformational.

To my relief, not too much later, Lori and the girls came home, and my attention was immediately brought back to the package. I wanted to tear it open.

Lori wasn't in a hurry. She said she had a million things to do.

Over the past couple weeks, she had gotten most of her energy back and said she was feeling, as she put it, "close to normal." But I sensed she was just as excited to open the package as I was. She just wanted to play it cool.

So, after about ten minutes of darting in and out of the family room, she plopped down on the couch beside me.

> I could honestly say my Truest Fan commitment was continuing to be transformational.

"You've been a good boy," she cooed. "I know how hard it must have been to wait a whole two hours to open that package."

"C'mon," I shot back, "I can see you're excited too."

When I peeled back the wrapping, I was stunned. I discovered a framed picture of the Indians' jumbotron that included Lori's photo with the Truest Fan get-well wishes. The same image I had seen at the stadium on the day of my Truest Fan graduation.

The only differences were the engraving underneath the photo, *Lori is now cancer-free*, and a date from the previous week.

Too stunned to say anything, I just sat there with a huge smile and a very puzzled look on my face.

Lori broke the silence.

"Surprise!" she exclaimed. "Thank you for being my Truest Fan. I couldn't have beaten cancer without you."

"I'm so happy for you," I responded, "but how is this possible? Did you put my Truest Fans friends up to this?"

"No," she quickly admitted, "I did it myself. I couldn't think of a better way to tell you. I found out last week and I already had the idea of framing this picture for you. I just needed to add the inscription and date and then I mailed to our house."

"You wouldn't believe how difficult it's been for me to keep this a secret from you."

"And there's more," she added before I had a chance to say anything. "Do you remember that epic trip we've been talking about? Wondering if I'd be healthy enough to travel?"

"Well, I am. And I'm taking our whole family to Spring Training. Two weeks of sunshine, Tribe baseball and, most importantly, time with our family."

"And we'll have a lot to celebrate too," I added.

"Yes, we will," she agreed.

# THE
# 7 LESSONS
# OF TRUEST FAN
# WISDOM

Download your free copy of my
**Truest Fan Implementation Guide**
at **truestfan.com/free**

# LESSON #1

## To be a Truest Fan, you must be your own Truest Fan.

"Let go of self–doubt and become your
own truest fan because the life that
you're living is the life God intends for
you to live. He's blessing you. You need to
accept his blessings with open arms."

—Bruiser

# LESSON #2

**To be a Truest Fan, you must learn to put your most important work first and avoid anything that may get in the way.**

"We live in a world where it's easy to put other people's agendas ahead of our own. We allow ourselves to become distracted by text messages, emails and phone calls. We surrender our time to others. We need to put our most important priorities ahead of our daily distractions."

—Ken

# LESSON #3

## Love one another because no matter whether you win or lose, life is about the way you play the game.

"We're not meant to do things just so others can see us. We're really built so that others see God through the things that we do. When we trust God that way, the good gifts that we share are multiplied exponentially."

—Jack

# LESSON #4

## Smiles and kind words go a long way. When you're a Truest Fan, you're always on duty.

"You never know when a smile, a wink, a nod, a hello or a word of encouragement touches someone's life in a way that lasts forever. And at the very least, those smiles and kind words have a compounding effect on others."

—Willie

# LESSON #5

## Your family deserves your very best.

"You need to be a Truest Fan of your spouse and your family. They totally deserve the best of everything you're doing for yourself and for others."

—Sue

# LESSON #6

## You are never alone.
## God is your Truest Fan.

"God is your Truest Fan through thick and thin. And just like the rest of us, all he really asks is that you do your best to be his Truest Fan too."

—John-Patrick

# LESSON #7

## Intentionally live the life you were intended to live.

"There is no limit to the good we can do if we constantly remember to do the things we say we are going to do. If we turn our words, lessons and wisdom into action."

—Bruiser

# ABOUT THE AUTHOR

Hello, my name is Rob Brown. Much of my career has been spent in the financial services industry as a top-producing advisor followed by several senior leadership roles. Now, in addition to being an author, I'm an executive coach who helps my clients, financial professionals, and business leaders achieve excellence while living more purpose-filled lives.

Over the course of my career, I have discovered that a large part of my success has come through the active encouragement of others. Whether I'm coaching, mentoring, speaking, or leading training events, I love cheering on colleagues and clients.

*Truest Fan* distills ways of thinking, acting and doing so you can perform at your highest level while encouraging others to do the same.

You will follow the journey of 7 characters who each convey lessons you can put into practice in your business as well as in life. Just as in baseball, before you reach the major leagues, you need to develop success habits . . . daily rituals and routines in which you engage to reach your biggest goals.

This book helps focus your attention on what matters most in your life—be it a spouse, business, colleagues, or kids. Many people lose years of their life because of the intensity of urgent to-dos and the distractions we all face.

*Truest Fan* strips back this facade. It helps you consider what your life would be like if you were purposely living each day as your own Truest Fan. Think about it . . . what would your life be like if you were to swing for the fences in each relationship, each project, and each goal?

It might amaze you to find that you would begin to win more games. And along the way you would enjoy the journey a whole lot more!

If you enjoyed this book and found it helpful, please leave a REVIEW on Amazon.

Visit us at **www.truestfan.com**
where you can sign up for email updates.